Growth, Profit and Long Range Planning in Banks

Research for Business Decisions, No. 12

Other Titles in This Series

No. 11 Commercial Banks and the Creditworthiness of Less Developed Countries	Yoon-Dae Euh
No. 13 Strategies of U.S. Independent Oil Companies Abroad	Jean-Francois G. Landeau
No. 14 Bank Credit Cards for EFTS: A Cost-Benefit Analysis	Robert W. McLeod
No. 15 Uses of Financial Information in Bank Lending Decisions	Ray G. Stephens
No. 16 Understanding Personality and Motives of Women Managers	Harish C. Tewari
No. 17 Plant Location Decisions of Foreign Manufacturing Investors in the U.S.	Hsin-Min Tong

Growth, Profit and Long Range Planning in Banks

by
Hans E. Klein

RESEARCH PRESS

Produced and distributed by
University Microfilms International
Ann Arbor, Michigan 48106

Library of Congress Cataloging in Publication Data

Klein, Hans Emil, 1939-
Growth, profit and long range planning in banks.

(Research for business decisions ; no. 12)
Bibliography: p.
Includes index.
1. Bank management. 2. Banks and banking—Planning.
3. Banks and banking—United States. I. Title. II. Series.

HG1615.K54 658'.91'33212 79-24717
ISBN 0-8357-1051-3

TABLE OF CONTENTS

CONTENTS

ILLUSTRATIONS

TABLES

TABLES

TABLES

ACKNOWLEDGMENTS

I wish to express my sincere appreciation to those who made this study possible. To the members of my dissertation committee, Dr. James A. Knoblett, Dr. Levis D. McCullers, Dr. Joseph L. Massie, and Dr. Russel Brannon for their support and cooperation during the course of the study.

I wish to give special recognition to Dr. Don L. Madden, chairman of the dissertation committee. He provided guidance, encouragement, and competent supervision throughout the project. His professional and unselfish efforts were an inspiration and a major factor in bringing this dissertation to completion.

A special acknowledgment is due to the bank officers, controllers, and officials in the United States and West Germany who were interviewed during the field research for this study and to all bankers who completed the questionnaire. Their enthusiastic cooperation made this phase of the study very rewarding and enjoyable.

I am indebted to the Bank Administration Institute for awarding a Doctoral Research Grant and for providing invaluable technical support.

To my friends and teachers who have extended inspiration, encouragement, and assistance over the years, I profess my sincere thanks, especially to Dr. Jens R. Lindemann and Herbert Freedmann.

To my parents, whose pride in my accomplishments has always served as a motivating force, I express my love and gratitude for making me cognizant of the value of a formal education, and for their support and never ending faith.

Finally, I wish to express my deepest appreciation and love to my spouse, Emmi, for her many sacrifices made on my behalf. Her faith, encouragement and patient understanding contributed immensely to this research project.

CHAPTER I

INTRODUCTION

The general belief among businessmen is that a well-managed firm (bank) does not haphazardly achieve a certain profit level, but that profits are rather a result of extensive planning efforts. McCullers and Van Daniker (1975) explain that planning for profits, to be meaningful, must be achieved in view of all considerations within the firm. They further state:

> Inherent in the planning process is the forecast of events occurring in the future and their impact on the firm. These forecasts normally include projections of:
>
> 1. The economy, both short-run and long-run, and its impact on the industry and the firm.
> 2. Market analysis of the type and volume of sales for the industry and the firm.
> 3. The nature of competition, both within and outside the industry.
> 4. Production capabilities [bank facilities].
> 5. Labor and material availability [manpower].[1]

Although planning is believed to be of considerable importance to the progress of commercial banks, little empirical evidence has been collected to ascertain the impact of long range planning.

The purpose of this study is to investigate the following:

a) What is the relationship between bank size and long range planning efforts undertaken

b) What is the relationship between bank size and trends for growth and profit

c) Is there a correlation between

   1. the extent of long range planning and growth trends

   2. the extent of long range planning and profit trends

   3. the extent of long range planning, bank size and trends for growth and profit

d) To what extent is long range planning used as a management tool in commercial banks today.

Scope of the Study

Methodology

A questionnaire (refer to Appendix A) was used to collect the data necessary to achieve the above stated goals. The responses to the questionnaire were used to classify the participating banks as follows:

a) vertically, according to bank size, as measured by total average deposits during 1970, and

b) Horizontally, according to the extent of long range planning activities undertaken by the bank, as determined by a "long range planning score" attained by the bank. (Refer to the definition of the "long range planning score" in this Chapter).

The resulting classification design is illustrated below.

Figure I-1

Research-Partition-Design

Bank-Size	LRP-ACTIVITIES		
	HIGH	MODERATE	LOW
A	cell 1	cell 2	cell 3
B	cell 4	cell 5	cell 6
C	cell 7	cell 8	cell 9

The specific goals of the study are to test several sets of hypotheses and to determine the extent to which commercial banks use long range planning as a management tool. Data relating to growth and profit are used to test hypotheses designed to examine the following areas of relationships:

1. Bank size and extent of long range planning efforts undertaken

2. Bank size and trends for growth and profit

3. Extent of long range planning and trends for growth and profit

4. Extent of long range planning, bank size, and trends for growth and profit.

The data analysis will provide answers to the following questions:

— whether the extent of long range planning undertaken by banks increases when bank size increases or decreases;

— whether the extent of long range planning undertaken by banks decreases when bank size increases or decreases;

— whether bank size affects (increases or decreases) growth trends in banks;

— whether bank size affects (increases or decreases) profit trends in banks;

— whether different degrees in long range planning efforts (high, moderate, low) undertaken by banks of the same size are correlated with differences in growth and profit changes, e.g., whether banks that engage in low long range planning efforts have lower growth and profit increases than banks that engage in moderate or high long range planning efforts.

Definitions

Some key terms used in this study are briefly defined in the section that follows. Comprehensive definitions and explanations are included in Appendix B.

1. Long range planning.

In the context of this study, long range planning encompasses all planning activities that exceed a time horizon of one year. Essentially all factors considered in the development of short range plans are included. Variations between short and long range plans primarily involve differences in accuracy and detail, in greater orientation toward planning rather than control, and in greater awareness of environmental changes.

2. Extent of long range planning.

The extent of long range planning efforts undertaken by the bank was determined through interviews and information collected through the questionnaire used in this study. A long range planning score was computed for each respondent.

3. Functional Cost Analysis Program.

The Functional Cost Analysis program is a joint effort of all Federal Reserve Banks and their member banks. Participation in the program is voluntary. The major purpose of the Functional Cost Analysis program is to provide an extensive evaluation of bank operations through the analysis of bank functions. This goal is accomplished through the development of a uniform cost accounting system for use by the member banks as a management tool. Refer to Chapter III for a detailed description and discussion of the Functional Cost Analysis program and how it is used in this study.

4. Bank size.

Using total average deposits for the year 1970, all participating banks were classified into one of three groups:

a) Banks with total deposits of up to $50 million (Class C)

b) Banks with total deposits from $50 million to $200 million (Class B)

c) Banks with total deposits of more than $200 million (Class A).

5. Growth.

Data on changes of average total deposits were used as surrogates for growth trends of the participating banks. Functional Cost Analysis data were used. For more detail refer to Appendix B.

6. Profit.

Net Yield after Cost of Cash, as defined and used in the Functional Cost Analysis program, served as surrogates for profit trends. For more detail refer to Chapter IV.

Limitations

The limitations of this study arise from two sources. First, a bank, under normal conditions, offers customers a large number of diversified products and services.[2] A discussion and inclusion of all these products and services into the research design of this study is neither feasible nor necessary and desirable because of the wide range of variations in "product-service mix" among commercial banks and the limited resources available to one researcher. The focus of this study, therefore, is limited to the main "contributor" to overall bank profit, the loan-deposit-investment function.

Second, other limitations arise from the selection of the Functional Cost Analysis reports as data base for this study. The Functional Cost Analysis data, however, have the distinct advantage of being derived from uniform standards and procedures. Among the available data sources, the Functional Cost Analysis data are the only set of data that permit meaningful comparisons among a large number of banks of different sizes. The limitations set forth above are developed further in Chapter IV.

Organization of the Study

The preceding sections have presented an overview of the rationale of this study. The methodology was developed and specific goals of the project were discussed. Key terms were briefly explained and basic limitations of the project were presented.

Chapter II describes the economic environment of commercial banks, the need for profits and growth, and the search for ways to maintain adequate profits and growth levels. A characterization of the banking environment in the United States follows. Chapter II concludes with a discussion of the applicability of long range planning in the banking sector.

The purpose of Chapter III is to explain the Functional Cost Analysis program, its rationale, advantages, and disadvantages. An in-depth evaluation of the use of the Functional Cost Analysis is included in the same chapter.

The methodology used in the study is developed in detail in Chapter IV. Questionnaire, sample, long range planning scores, research partition design, data arrangement and computations, statistics employed, testing of the hypotheses, and procedures used in the analysis of long range planning questions are discussed.

Chapter V presents the analysis of the data gathered and tests of the hypotheses. The data are tested for significant statisitical differences through use of the Analysis of Variance procedure.

A summary of the study, the conclusions and interpretations derived from this empirical research are presented in Chapter VI. The chapter includes a discussion of suggestions for further research.

The Appendix of the study contains copies of the questionnaire and cover letter mailed to all respondents, information relating to definitions of key terms used in this study, a computation of "long range planning scores" used for classification purposes, and an analysis of the long range planning questions used in the questionnaire. Procedural discussions of the geometric mean and analysis of variance follow. A compilation of the answers received in response to the questionnaires concludes the Appendix.

CHAPTER II

UNITED STATES BANKING AND ITS ENVIRONMENT

Introduction

This chapter provides a framework for this study by reviewing important characteristics of recent developments in the field of banking in the United States. The economic environment of banks and the need for profit and growth are discussed.

The recent history of banking is briefly traced, and is followed by a discussion of Financial Intermediaries. A section on the Dual Banking System presents information on Federal and State regulations, the Federal Reserve Bank System, the FDIC, bank-branching, mergers, and bank-holding companies.

The salient features of the banking environment, Fractional Reserve System, economic developments, competition, changes in technology, are also described. Remarks on the importance and applicability of long range planning in the commercial banking industry conclude the chapter.

Economic Environment

Traditionally, the United States banking system has been composed of a large number of independent banks, serving the local needs of local customers.[3] The great majority of American banks are relatively small. Despite their numbers, these commercial banks provide a smoothly functioning banking service.

> They [commercial banks] perform a wide range of community services which relate to their primary function of making loans and investments and handling bank deposits in a money economy in which the greater part of transactions are effected through the exchange of bank deposits.[4]

The past several decades of commercial banking in the United States have seen change and growth. Olson (1964) states the following reasons for this development:

> First, a widespread acceptance of branch banking and consolidations and mergers of unit banks has contributed to the complexity of the commercial banking system; second, there has been a growth of competition from other financial institutions, such as savings and loan associations, savings banks, and credit unions; and third, modern day communication and transportation patterns have brought much intra-industry competition.[5]

Table II-1

Commercial Banks in the United States, 1835-1966, Selected Years[a]

Year[b]	State banks[c]	National banks	Private banks[d]
1835	704		
1840	901		
1850	824		
1855	1,307		
1861	1,601		
1862	1,492		
1864	1,089	467	
1865	349	1,294	
1867	272	1,636	
1868	247	1,640	
1870	325	1,612	
1875	586	2,076	
1885	1,015	2,689	3,456
1890	2,250	3,484	4,305
1895	4,369	3,715	3,924
1900	5,007	3,731	5,187
1910	14,348	7,138	3,669
1915	17,748	7,597	2,737
1925	19,573	8,066	915
1930	15,798	7,247	598
1933	8,908	4,987	330
1935	9,752	5,425	246
1940	9,181	5,164	57
1950	9,163	4,958	
1955	9,024	4,692	
1960	8,942	4,530	
1963	8,954	4,615	
1966	8,971	4,799	

Source: William J. Brown, *The Dual Banking System in the United States* (New York: The American Bankers Association, 1968), p. 14, 15. Refer to footnotes following.

[a]Data for the years 1835-1940 selected from Board of Governors of the FRS, *Banking Studies* (Baltimore: Waverly Press, Inc., 1941), pp. 418 and 419; for the years 1945-1966, data compiled by the Board of Governors of the FRS and published in current issues of the *Federal Reserve Bulletin.* (Includes noninsured banks.)

[b]All figures for the years 1935-1940 are as of June 30, or nearest available date; for the years 1945-1966, data are as of December 31.

Table II-1 (Continued)

[c]Excludes mutual savings banks. Includes unincorporated banks for the years 1945-1966.

[d]Data for years prior to 1877 are not available. Because of their small and diminishing number, figures for these banks for the years 1945-1966 are included in the state bank column.

This change and growth in banking did not bring an immediate concern for changes in management approaches, especially in the area of planning. Reierson (1964) attributes this to the fact that "lead-times" have not played the same role in banks as they did in industry.

> Planning seems to have had an earlier development in industry than in banking. In industry, where fairly long lead-times are involved in adding plant capacity, the need to look ahead has long been recognized. For a great many years commercial banks, in contrast, did not appear to have an important problem in this area.[6]

During the period from 1943 to 1962 commercial banks earned profits which were considered reasonable in terms of return on shareholder's equity, and trending upward in terms of dollars.[7] This favorable profit experience is believed to be one of the explanations for the lag in adopting profit planning techniques by commercial banks. Further explanations may be found in the reluctance and unwillingness to change old habits, as well as in the lack of expertise in this area of management.

Need for Profit and Growth

During the period from 1956 through 1962, however, an important economic change took place.[8] Banks experienced a decline in profits relative to profit trends of other industries.[9] This trend continued through the entire decade as is evidenced by data supplied in Table II-2.

Banks gross profit margins dropped by half in 17 years, from 37 percent in 1955 to 18 percent in 1972.[10] Many factors contributed to the increase in bank cost: the use of high cost sources of funds, the growth of time deposits as a percentage of liabilities, and the increasing turnover rates of demand deposits. At the same time, banks' interest rates on loans were held down by usury laws and consumer price resistance.

Furthermore, competition among bankers took on an aggressiveness comparable to that found in other industries. Bank managers thus realized that if banks were going to be important financial institutions in

Table II-2

Ratios of income—Insured Commercial Banks (amounts per $100 of current operating revenue)

Year	Current Operating Revenue Total	Current Operating Expense Total	Net Current Operating Earnings
1961	$100.00	$67.22	$32.78
1962	100.00	70.29	29.71
1963	100.00	71.91	28.09
1964	100.00	72.53	27.47
1965	100.00	74.25	25.75
1966	100.00	74.64	25.36
1967	100.00	76.00	24.00
1968	100.00	75.96	24.04
1969	100.00	78.15	21.85
1970	100.00	79.47	20.53

Source: Federal Deposit Insurance Corporation, *Annual Reports*, Washington, D.C.

the future, they had to meet the challenge to compete for adequate profit over the long run.

The growth of industrial business prompted the development of larger banks in order to meet the needs of large business customers. Expansion of banking size provided larger lending limits to handle the credits required by large business. Expansion was also motivated by the need for reducing operating costs and for efficient handling of the numerous financial transactions of large industrial corporations. Of course, some of this growth in size was accomplished through the merger of existing banks.

Profits are necessary to meet the expectations of shareholders for dividends and for continued growth. Inadequate profits not only limit an industry's ability to grow, but they also tend to inhibit progressiveness in that industry.[11]

These points are further emphasized by Haskins & Sells, Certified Public Accountants, in a study on "Bank Cost for Planning and Control" which they prepared for the Bank Administration Institute.

> The dynamic, well-managed bank—one that is efficient and profitable—offers society an important public service. Conversely, the bank that is not well-managed is likely to be unprofitable and a threat to the financial health of the community it serves.
>
> As a result, society has an interest in the efforts of bank managers who run their banks to benefit not only the owners and investors but also the public that depends heavily on bank services.[12]

Inadequacy of profits can have serious consequences. An industry which is subject to a level of profits consistently less than adequate cannot survive. Laudadio (1960) found that survival is a prime consideration for banks.

> . . . because in the United States the prevailing feeling is for a private banking system and strongly against nationalization, the banking industry, as now organized, is vital to the American economy, and nothing which endangers its survival should be allowed to exist.[13]

The Federal Reserve System has given explicit recognition to the fact that the level of commercial bank earnings has a bearing on the long-run stability of the financial structure of the nation.[14] Banks provide many vital services to our society. Their survival through sustained profits is thus a key element for a continued high standard of living in the United States.

A dramatic increase in the internationalization of commerce since World War II resulted in greater interdependency of developed and developing nations. Actions in one country have what economists call "spill-over" effects in other countries. The stability of the United States banking system thus has implications that transcend national boundaries.

Search for Solution

The decline in profits and the increase in competition prompted bank executives to look for new and better techniques of management. In 1958, Sord and Welsch praised as the most significant development in scientific management within recent years, the increasing recognition of the importance of long range planning.[15] Subsequently, during the mid 1960's, several studies suggested that profit planning techniques and long range planning, frequently used in other industries (mainly manufacturing), could also be applied successfully to commercial banking.[16, 17]

Planning is a basic function of the management process and provides the foundation upon which the other management functions operate.[18] Steiner (1962) defines long range planning as

> . . . the conscious determination of courses of action to achieve preconceived objectives. It [planning] is deciding in advance what is to be done, and how it is to be done. It can range from the detailed, specific, and rigid to the broad, general, and flexible design. Long-range planning does this for extended periods of time. Long-range planning is a process for establishing long-range goals, working out strategies, programs, and policies to achieve these goals; and setting up the necessary machinery to insure that the company gets where it wants to go. It is a process of choosing from alternative courses of action and charting the use of time, resources, and effort to achieve the objective sought. The further into the future the plan stretches the less detailed are its specific parts. The subject matter of long-range plans should cover products, services, facilities, manpower, research and development, organization, marketing, financial matters, and various aspects of management itself.[19, 20]

Bank management is judged to a large extent by its ability to earn an adequate return on investment. Anthony and Dearden (1965) state

> The predominant goal of banking is the attainment of long-term success through earning a reasonable rate of return for the investors along with satisfactory performance in certain other "key result areas."[21]

Whether or not a profit is "adequate" is decided by considering it in relation to the industry experience and the general business environment.[22]

No bank can isolate itself from the long range consequences of actions taken or not taken during a period. Therefore, a plan should not be considered desirable or undesirable only on the basis of its short-term impact. The short range planner almost inevitably seems to develop an orientation toward small, gradual changes. Many times the perspective provided by long range planning is necessary to reveal the larger dimension of change and the action required to meet this change.

Despite an abundance of general literature on profit planning and the recognition of its importance in other industries, literature on its use in banking is sparse. The Bank Administration Institute (1959) and Hegazy and Blakely (1966)[23, 24] published studies on planning and budgets. However, Federal Regulatory Agencies and Institutions, such as the Federal Reserve System, the Federal Deposit Insurance Corporation, and the Comptroller of the Currency, maintain no statistical data on banks formally recognizing the existence of profit planning programs. Therefore, no comparisons of the profitability of banks with such a program to those without one have been undertaken.[25, 26]

Extensive discussions and interviews with bankers at local, state, national and international levels confirmed that bankers generally believe that the larger the bank, the more extensive are the long range planning efforts undertaken by the bank. Extensive planning efforts in turn are thought to result in higher profit and growth trends. Little, if any, empirical data exist to support this claim.

Fulmer and Rue (1973) found a similar paucity of empirical data when examining long range planning and profit trends in three selected industry groups (non-durables, durables, services). They noted that

> . . . in spite of the increased emphasis on long-range planning, the great majority of the planning literature deals specifically with how to plan. Very little empirical research has been conducted to determine relationships between long-range planning and performance of the firm.[27]

Recent History of U.S. Banking

As pointed out earlier, the banking system in the United States, traditionally, has been composed of a large number of independent banks. In other countries, notably in Germany, France, Canada, and Great Britain, relatively few large branch systems are spread across the entire nation. The great majority of American banks are relatively small. They have grown with their communities. Despite their numbers, they provide a smoothly functioning banking service. Their primary services are handling bank deposits and making loans and investments. Over the years many different types of services have been added as banks adapted to the lifestyles and financial needs of their customers.

Commercial banks stand at the crossroads of the nation's commerce. They create and hold the money supply, execute the transfer of funds arising from business and personal transactions, hold a large part of the savings and supply a large part of the credit needed for the economy to function smoothly.

The term "commercial bank" was first used in Great Britain over a hundred years ago, when most banks that accepted demand deposits limited their loans to those for short term commercial purposes.[28] Commercial banks, as distinguished from other financial intermediaries, are the only financial institutions that are allowed to accept demand deposits which are transferable to third parties by check. These checking deposits represent the major part of the country's money supply.

The health of commercial banks and the continued well-being of the nation are inextricable intertwined because of the central role that banks play in the United States economy. Most changes in banking in the past two decades have their origins in fundamental economic trends.[29]

To some extent, changes of the last several decades have been a recovery from the shocks of the Depression and World War II.[30] In other respects, some of the recent events in banking represent evolutionary changes, as banks adapted to changes in their environment. Widespread acceptance of branch banking, consolidations resulting from the growth of other financial institutions, and modern day communications and transportation patterns have done much to change the banking industry.[31] In addition, public policy, expressed and enforced by State and Federal Regulatory Agencies, has provided a strong and constant influence throughout this era.

Most businessmen agree that planning holds a central place in a company's ability to adapt to such changes. Many businessmen and bankers also agree that long range planning is a vital activity within a firm or bank. How vital long range planning activities in banking are, however, and how extensive they need to be, has not yet been determined. One purpose of this study, therefore, is to provide answers to these questions.

Financial Intermediaries

Commercial banks are one of the major types of financial intermediaries in the United States. Some of the others are financial businesses such as savings and loan associations, mutual savings banks, credit unions, insurance companies and finance companies. These intermediaries serve as "exchange" centers of funds. Surplus funds are collected from customers and distributed to other customers.[32]

In the United States economy, a substantial part of all credit goes through intermediaries. Table II-3 below shows 1972 data on supply and demand for credit. The left-hand column lists the financial intermediaries which play major roles in supplying credit to the U.S. economy. The right-hand column indicates the total amount of credit supplied by each intermediary.

Commercial banks supplied $70 billion of a total of $182.5 billion, or 38.4 percent; the second largest supplier of credit, savings and loan associations, supplied $35.8 billion, or 19.6 percent. (It should be noted that these are net figures—new credits supplied less repayments or retirements.) The users of credit and the types of credit investments involved in obtaining credit from the various financial intermediaries are indicated across the top of the table. Examination of the data presented indicates that commercial banks and savings and loan assoiations are the main suppliers of credit.

The Dual Banking System

Banking in the United States is characterized by a unique feature:

Table II-3

Supply and Demand for Credit, Calendar Year 1972 (Billions of Dollars)

	U.S. Government Securities		*Mortgages*		*Corporate Securities*		*State & Local Government Securities*	*Consumer Loans*	*Business Loans*	*Open Market Paper*	*Other Bank Loans*	*Foreign Securities*	*Total*
	Direct	*Agency*	*Home*	*Other*	*Bonds*	*Stocks*							
Life Insurance Company	-0.1	–	-2.6	3.8	6.7	3.6	–	0.9	–	0.8	–	0.3	13.4
Fire and Casualty Insurance	–	-0.1	–	–	0.3	2.6	3.3	–	–	–	–	0.1	6.2
Savings and Loan Association	1.6	1.7	24.2	7.9	–	–	–	0.1	–	0.3	–	–	35.8
Mutual Savings Banks	0.1	1.5	2.8	2.7	2.2	0.5	0.5	0.3	–	–	–	–	10.6
Credit Unions	1.2	–	0.1	–	–	–	–	2.1	–	–	–	–	3.4
Commercial Banks	1.7	1.5	7.8	8.6	1.6	–	8.1	10.1	20.2	-0.8	11.2	–	70.0
Corporate Pension Funds	0.2	0.2	–	-0.7	-0.3	6.7	–	–	–	–	–	–	6.1
State and Local Pension Funds	0.2	-0.3	–	-0.1	4.4	2.8	-0.3	–	–	–	–	0.5	7.2
Mutual Funds	–	–	–	–	0.2	-1.6	–	–	–	–	–	–	-1.4
Nonfinancial Corps	1.0	0.5	–	–	–	–	-0.4	3.3	–	0.8	–	–	5.2
Financial Companies	–	–	3.3	–	–	–	–	3.2	1.4	–	–	–	7.9
Foreigners	8.6	0.1	–	–	0.2	1.9	–	–	–	-0.2	–	–	10.6
State and Local Government	2.8	1.0	–	–	–	–	–	–	–	0.3	–	–	4.1
Individuals and Miscellaneous	-3.3	3.6	-3.0	3.8	4.1	-2.7	1.3	–	–	-0.4	–	–	3.4
Totals	14.0	9.7	32.6	26.0	19.4	13.8	12.5	20.0	21.6	0.8	11.2	0.9	182.5

Source: Salomon Brothers; Supply and Demand for Credit in 1973, as derived from Flow of Funds data of the Federal Reserve.

the concept of dual banking. The dual banking system enables banks to operate either under the authority of the state in which they are chartered or under the authority of the federal government. A uniquely American product, the dual banking system has its foundation in the delegation of governmental sovereignty[33] among the states and the federal government.[34]

Federal and State Regulations

For banks now operating under state charters, the significance of dual banking lies in the ability to obtain a national charter in the event that state supervision and regulation should become unduly oppressive, arbitrary, or discriminatory. For the banks now operating under national charters, dual banking offers the same safeguard against the emergence of oppressive, arbitrary, or discriminatory regulation at the Federal level. However, the option of switching from a national to a state charter is contingent on the avoidance of any adverse effect on the bank's insured status.[35]

Today, the commercial banking system in the United States embraces more than 14,000 separate banks. Almost 6,000 of these banks are chartered by the federal government as national banks, while the remainder are chartered by the states.[36] These 14,000 banks conduct business with the public as well as with local, state, and federal government. They accept deposits and lend to individuals, businesses and governments.

Federal Reserve System and FDIC

The Federal Reserve Bank is one of the Federal Agencies supervising and regulating commercial banks. In order to serve all parts of the country adequately and avoid an overconcentration of money power in any institution, the Federal Reserve Act of 1913 set up twelve Federal Reserve districts, each with a Federal Reserve Bank. (The Federal Reserve bank system is the equivalent of the Central Bank in other countries.) The system was established to accomplish the following: (1) to make the nation's monetary and banking system more sound and efficient, and (2) to correct one of the major weaknesses of the 1864 National Banking Act: the financial instability created by that system.

Although the National Banking Act of 1864 brought a marked improvement to the nation's banking system, it still has serious imperfections. Among them were: (1) The Central Banks were a system in name only. There was no centralization, unification, or coordination. There was no provision for the collection or clearing of checks. (2) Unsatisfactory basis of reserves. Many reserves were fictitious. Serious problems were created in times of economic contraction through the practice of holding some reserves in form of balances with other banks and permitting the expansion of bank credit when business was good.

The Federal Reserve System was specifically created to fulfill three principal functions:

1. to hold member bank reserves;

2. to serve as a "lender of last resort" for banks in temporary need of liquidity;

3. to provide a more orderly process for the clearing of checks, particularly over long distances.

Since World War II, the control of the money supply as a means of stabilizing the economy has emerged as a major function of the Federal Reserve Bank. Two main tools at the disposal of the Federal Reserve Bank are used to achieve stabilization: (1) The ability to raise or lower percentage reserve requirements of member banks; (2) The ability to increase or decrease its own holdings of government (or other) securities through trading in the open market. The Federal Reserve Bank pays for these securities with checks drawn upon itself which, when deposited by the recipient, represent new bank reserves. This increase in reserves then releases deposits for lending activities.

The Federal Reserve System did not take the place of the National Banking System, but was superimposed on it. The American system of many thousands of independent banks was continued. The new system was designed to federate them into a unified system, democratic in its organization and nationwide in its field of operation.[37]

Membership in the Federal Reserve System is compulsory for national banks and voluntary for state banks, which may join if they can satisfy membership requirements. Other state-chartered financial institutions, such as savings and loan associations, consumer finance companies, and credit unions, are not eligible for membership. Altogether, member banks account for 76 percent of all deposits of commercial banks.[38]

A further distinguishing characteristic among banks is whether or not their deposits are insured by the Federal Deposit Insurance Corporation. All Federal Reserve Bank members, and almost all state banks, are insured.[39]

Of the powers vested in regulatory agencies, those concerning reserve requirements are among the most important. Reserves are a fulcrum for the operation of monetary policy, and they exert an important influence on bank costs and liquidity.[40] All members of the Federal Reserve System are subject to reserve requirements and must hold their reserves as deposits with the regional Federal Reserve Bank, except for that portion represented by vault cash. With reference to the foregoing, state banks have advantages when compared with Federal Reserve members. However, there may be offsetting differences in other areas of time and savings deposits.

Traditionally, the pre-conditions for dual banking have been considered to be: (1) the existence of entry routes into commercial banking at both Federal and state levels, and (2) the freedom of existing banks to shift from one type of charter to another, thereby substituting one set of regulatory and supervisory standards for another.[41]

The dual banking system has changed considerably since it was created through the National Banking Act of 1864. Prior to the creation of the Federal Deposit Insurance Corporation, state and Federal governments regulated the entry of new banks into the commercial banking system.

Through the requirement of deposit insurance as a virtual necessity for new banks, the Federal Deposit Insurance Corporation has acquired a potential veto over entry into banking by new state-charted institutions which are not members of the Federal Reserve System. In addition, the Federal Reserve Bank can veto deposit insurance for banks which attempt to enter into the commercial banking system through the Federal Reserve membership route.

Regulation of entry into commercial banking is thus characterized by duality at the Federal level (FDIC and Federal Reserve Bank). This shift to the Federal level does not, however, negate the historical arguments in favor of dual chartering authority (state versus Federal government). Current institutional arrangements offer as much protection against discriminatory or arbitrary processing of charter applications as did exist under previous institutions.[42]

The preceding discussion of the Federal Reserve System and the FDIC is included to present the proper setting for this study. Because all the banks studied are federally chartered, the issue of charters and their effects on profit and growth in commercial banks is not important for this study. (Refer to Chapter IV for more detail.) For an in-depth discussion of the impact of Federal Reserve membership on profits in commercial banks refer to Lucille Stringer Mayne (1967).[43]

Branching, Mergers, Bank-holding Companies

Over the last several decades, branch banking has become an issue in some states. This trend started at the beginning of this century and became more widespread after the Depression, as a result of several moves to strengthen the financial system.

After World War II, urban banks followed their customers into the suburbs through acquisition of suburban banks. The tremendous increase in the number of consolidations which took place during the mid 1950's led to the passage of the Bank Merger Act of 1960. This Act, and several suits by the Justice Department against several large banks contemplating mergers, reflect the concern of Congress to protect the American banking system against overconcentration and monopoly.[44] More recently, the Justice Department raised antitrust objections to a proposed joint venture among commercial banks in Nebraska to develop a statewide electronic funds transfer system.[45]

Another method used to circumvent the restrictions against branch banking was the development of bankholding companies in many states. Holding companies were created to acquire the stock of several banks in one area (often a state). Common ownership led to common management teams and goals, and benefits comparable to those achieved through branching. In many instances, these holding companies expanded into other approved lines of business; e.g. investment advice, insurance sales, mortgage banking. Several Acts of Congress and guidelines issued by states are now regulating these companies as well.

Banking Environment

The following section will examine the effects of various aspects of the environment on commercial banking. Important features of the economic and competitive environment will be presented. A discussion of the regulatory system affecting commercial banks and the importance of technological changes will follow.

The banking environment is of considerable importance for this research project. Long range planning, the area of inquiry for this study, is one of the tools at management's disposal to provide for an orderly adaptation to changing conditions. The central place that profits hold in banks is well recognized (refer to discussion in Chapter I and II).

Stability of the banking system and, consequently, stability of the financial structure of the nation are at stake.

Fractional Reserve Banking

Demand deposits constitute the principal part of the U.S. money supply, and so commercial banks play a unique role in the financial system: they are the only financial intermediaries that are allowed to accept demand deposits transferable to third parties by check.

The United States, like most other countries, operates under a system of "fractional reserve banking." Basically that means that banks keep only a fraction of their deposits in cash (or similar reserves) and lend out the rest to borrowers. These loans create money for the banking system. A loan made to a borrower is deposited in his checking account. As the borrower spends the money by writing checks, the checks become deposits in a third party's bank account. After the bank has set aside a portion of the money as reserves, the rest is loaned again. This sequence of events continues and results in a situation in which the amount of money circulating in the banking system (currency plus demand deposits) is a constant multiple of the amount of reserves.[46]

The amount of money in circulation is controlled by the Federal Reserve Bank through the formulation of monetary policy. To a certain degree, then, the aggregate growth of commercial banks' assets and liabilities is determined by Federal Reserve Board policies.

Economic Developments

As pointed out earlier, the past several decades of commercial banking in the United States have seen changes and growth, particularly the period since World War II. Except for a few relatively mild recessions, the years from 1945 through 1975 represent one of the longest periods of unbroken growth in U.S. history. Financial services and banking have been among the more rapidly growing sectors of the economy.

Among the many developments in banking during this time period, Teplitz (1976) lists the following as being especially significant:

1. a large growth in the aggregate assets and liabilities of banks;

2. shifts in the composition of both assets and liabilities;

3. change in the goal emphasis by bank managements from finding profitable uses for funds toward finding new sources of funds;

4. a decline in the ratio of bank capital to deposits;

5. a margin squeeze between the rates banks must pay for funds and the rates they can earn on them;

6. a persistent inflation which reinforces some of the above trends and creates problems in its own right.[47]

This combination of developments has caused some public concern about the continued health of the banking system and thus about its ability to fulfill its important role in our society. Adequacy of bank capital and the directly related capacity to absorb losses are being scrutinized more carefully.[48]

Competition

In addition to competing among themselves, banks face direct or indirect competition from all other financial intermediaries. Most prominent among the competitors of the commercial banks are the "thrift" institutions, mutual savings banks, savings and loan associations, and credit unions. Some of the other financial institutions that may compete with the commercial banks include finance companies, insurance companies, and brokerage firms. (Refer to Table II-3 in this chapter.)

The competition among rival financial intermediaries occurs in the following areas:

1. sources of funds;

2. uses of funds;

3. provision of a variety of services.

Competition for funds takes place most directly against other commercial banks, thrift institutions and direct investments. Competition in lending funds and rendering additional services occurs mainly against commercial banks, thrift institutions, consumer finance companies, life insurance companies, and brokerage houses. Direct credit instruments, such as commercial paper and business financing their own customers, are additional sources of competition.

Rival intermediaries specialize in some segments of the market, at least to some extent. Commercial banks, the most important group of the intermediaries,[49] compete in all segments of the market. Part of the specialization of the rival intermediaries is imposed by government regulations. Examples would be the dichotomy that exists between commercial banks and thrift institutions, or regulations that permit bank-holding companies to branch into non-intermediary services like investment counseling, mortgage banking, and insurance sales.

During the last twenty years, economic trends have changed the focus of bank competition from the uses of funds (lending) to the sources of funds (deposits, CDs, etc.). As a result of this shift, competitive strategies changed too. These strategies deal with such important issues as the evaluation of credit-worthiness of borrowers; business relations; branching; offering of new services to attract deposits; and servicing of consumer accounts. The last issue is particularly important since consumers are the greatest source of funds. In addition control of operating cost took on increased importance because of the high activity and low dollar volume of consumer accounts. A reduction in operating cost translated to a significant competitive advantage.

These changes did not occur overnight, but evolved over time. As a consequence, both short and long run projections became essential to assure timely adjustment to changing conditions in the environment. As an industry, commercial banks have managed a successful transition. During the last 15 years, they have held or increased their share of every major market segment they serve.[50]

Technological Changes

Banking procedures and banking technology have changed little until recently. The last decade has witnessed a tremendous technological change in commercial banks. Many clerical activities in banks are now being performed by computers and automated equipment.

During the 1950's and 1960's, banks mechanized a large portion of their operations. A recent survey[51] has shown that more than 50 percent of all commercial banks were automated, mostly for check processing and internal bookkeeping. Virtually all banks with more than $50 million in deposits are now automated. Among those banks not yet automated, more than four-fifths had less than $10 million deposits.

These developments are only the latest episode in the evolution of banking. Over decades, changes in the environment have improved methods of transportation and communication and have expanded the spheres of economic activity. Local boundaries have lost much of their significance. Most importantly, however, changes in expectations and needs of customers have brought about changes that further erase old boundaries and further blur the distinctions between commercial banks and other financial intermediaries.

When viewed in historical perspective, it is clear that structures, regulations, and traditions of the past have often lingered on, long beyond their relevance. Nevertheless, new financial institutions were created in response to new needs and new opportunities (National Banks, Federal Reserve Banks, Bank-holding companies, etc.). These events necessitated a re-evaluation of goals (some short-range, some long-range) and of the means and methods of achieving these goals.

Innovations in technology in banking are now causing changes in the competitive balance among institutions. These pressures, in time, will lead to a new "arrangement" of our financial system.

> The nature of future impacts of the technologies and the rapidity with which they come will depend on the outcomes of the long-continuing "tug of war" between the forces of localism, tradition, and specialization on the one hand and the forces of nationalism, modernism, and integration on the other. If history is a guide to the future, one must suppose that the forces of change, nationalism, and integration will eventually prevail.[52]

This developing "new system," in turn, will require adaptation and integration of goals. For the achievement of these goals, management might consider long range planning as an appropriate tool.

Several proposals for reform have been advanced over the years, and some laws have been passed. Concern about the need for a fundamental overhaul of the system has intensified recently.

The Commission on Money and Credit, a private group sponsored by the Committee for Economic Development (1958-1961) and, more recently, the President's Commission on Financial Structure and Regulation (known as the Hunt Commission), have undertaken thorough analyses of the regulation of financial markets. In general, they have recommended increasing competition among financial intermediaries by providing them with additional powers and greater operational freedom. Similar proposals have come from congressional committees.[53, 54]

Planning and Bank Management

One of the most important responsibilities of management (refer to discussion above) is to ensure the survival of the firm or organization, and survival can be guaranteed only through an adequate profit performance. In the long run, profits in any industry are not achieved haphazardly, but require careful planning and able execution of these plans.

Maintaining profits at a satisfactory level in a complex, constantly changing environment presents a tremendous challenge to the manager of a firm. Timely adjustments to changes become important. They may best be achieved through carefully designed and executed plans. Absence of long range planning activities may lead to deteriorating market position and declining profits, and may ultimately threaten the survival of the firm.

Bankers, like other business managers, are confronted with the often conflicting demands of many groups. The depositor wants a high return on his savings and low cost service on his checking account. The borrower desires an ample supply of credit at a minimum interest rate. The ever present shareholder wants a fair return on his investment, and bank employees continually demand higher wages. Competition is superimposed over all these demands, as are regulatory requirements by State and Federal Agencies.

A successful banker must be able to maximize his goals within the limits of prudent banking practices. If he can do this, his chances of reconciling the individual needs of these diverse groups are greatly enhanced. Trends in lending rates and the increased cost of deposits have forced the banker to look closely at the costs which are reducing profits. If he wishes to increase profits, the banker must not only manage assets wisely but also must be able to manage operations efficiently.

Bankers, like other business managers, thus face the same or similar challenges in terms of planning for their corporations' performance and survival. At times, there may be differences in the emphasis placed on selected segments of the company, differences caused by the environment or the peculiarity of the business. In essence, however, the tasks faced by management are the same in any industry.

In view of the above, therefore, it is more than justified to discuss and explore the applicability of management techniques, such as long range planning, in commercial banks. The question that faces the long range planner, wherever he may be, is not what his organization should do tomorrow but rather what it must do today to be ready for an uncertain tomorrow.

Summary

The survey of the pertinent literature has revealed that profits play a very important role in the banking industry; in fact, adequate profits are a precondition for the continued existence of the banking industry in its present form. During the past several decades the banking industry has gone through a period of change and growth; however, rising expenditures and keener competition affected profit margins to such an extent that banking executives started to search for new management techniques to increase profits, or at least to prevent profits from falling below satisfactory levels. Several studies suggested that planning techniques, successfully used in other industries, could be applied in commercial banks to help solve the problem that declining profits present for the banking industry and the economy as a whole.

No firm, no matter to which industry it belongs, can isolate itself any longer from the long range influence of actions taken or not taken during a period. One purpose of this study is to determine whether success, represented by profit and growth trends, is correlated to the extent of long range planning efforts undertaken by the bank. Most businessmen believe that such a correlation exists, although little, if any, empirical research has been conducted to support this claim.

The banking system in the United States is composed of a large number of independent banks. Although the great majority of them are relatively small, they provide a smoothly functioning banking service. Their primary services are handling bank deposits and making loans and investments.

The commercial bank is the major financial intermediary in the United States. In a recent year, such banks supplied 38.4 percent of all credit. The runner-up supplier of credit, savings and loan associations, had a share of 19.6 percent.

The banking system in the United States is characterized by the concept of dual banking. Banks can operate either under the authority of the state in which they were chartered or under the authority of the Federal Government. Two Federal Agencies, the Federal Reserve System and the Federal Deposit Insurance Corporation, exercise strong powers in regulating the financial institutions in the United States.

Over the years, commercial banking has changed because of economic developments, increased competition and advances in banking technology. In recent years, several proposals for a fundamental overhaul of the financial system have been advanced, but changes are taking place only slowly.

A key to the successful adaptation of commercial banks to changing conditions in the environment might be the use of long range planning as a management tool. Long range planning can be used in most management situations.

CHAPTER III

FUNCTIONAL COST ANALYSIS PROGRAM

Deposit and loan functions, the largest contributors to profit in commercial banks, are used as surrogates for the measurement of success in banks. (Success is represented by profit and growth trends.)

To guarantee accurate data for this study's measurements, the selection of a reliable data-base was critical. The most important criteria for a proper data-bank are consistently uniform data and feasibility of collection. Among the possible data-bases, the Functional Cost Analysis Program of the Federal Reserve System was the only data-bank that met these requirements for a large number of banks. In order to provide the background and rationale of these vital measurements, the Functional Cost Analysis Program is discussed in this chapter. This discussion takes on additional significance since no comprehensive description of the Functional Cost Analysis Program is available.

Chapter III contains a statement of the purpose of the Program as well as information on background and present use. Discussions of the data-base, fund concept, the structure of the annually published reports, and of the participating banks follows. Next, Fund Management and Fund Concepts used in the Banking Industry are presented. The chapter closes with a critical evaluation of the advantages and disadvantages of the Program as management tool and data-base for this study.

Purpose

The Functional Cost Analysis Program is a joint effort of the Federal Reserve Banks and their member banks. The Program's main purpose is to develop a uniform cost accounting system for use by members as a management tool. The Program develops functional income and cost data for individual banks and provides comparisons of these data within each bank from year to year and with other banks each year.

Because of differences in concepts, differences in degree of sophistication, and the heavy reliance on human judgment, confident comparison of one bank's costs with another's has been virtually impossible in the past. Frequently, even year-to-year comparisons within an individual bank were impractical.

The Functional Cost Analysis Program is a simplified, uniform system of cost accounting that entails only modest data collection and eliminates as many difficult judgments as possible. In those cases in which differences in methods of accounting cannot be eliminated by definitions or standard data collection procedures, adjustment techniques are applied uniformly in all participating banks.

Background and Present Use

The Federal Reserve Bank of Boston started the Functional Cost Analysis Program in 1957 with the goal of providing small and medium-sized banks with a technique for determining and monitoring their costs. The program spread rapidly to other Federal Reserve districts and is now used nationwide.

The Program enjoys widespread use not only among Federal Reserve System member banks but also among nonmember banks, analysts, and researchers (although it was not originally designed and developed as a research tool). Over the years, the Program has gained so good a reputation that Central Banks of other countries have inquired about the possibility of using an adapted version of the Program for their own member banks.[55]

The founder and present director[56] of the Functional Cost Analysis Program attributes the popularity and success of the Program to two facts. First, participation is voluntary; second, some effort is required on the part of the participating banks in terms of preparing and compiling input data and of analyzing the reports prepared by the Federal Reserve Banks for the member banks.

Prior to the development of the Functional Cost Analysis Program the Banking Industry lacked a uniform system of cost accounting that would require only modest data collection and would eliminate as many difficult judgments as possible without affecting the quality of the resulting reports adversely. This lack of uniformity of accounting systems has hampered previous studies exploring profits in commercial banks.

In 1962 Lynch researched the profitability of state-chartered member and non-member banks in Texas.[57] One of the more important criticisms of this study is the fact that no adjustment was made for variations in bank accounting practices, with consequent variations in reported profit.[58] The uniformity of the accounting system used by all participants (in the Functional Cost Analysis Program) makes the Functional Cost Analysis a strong research tool.

Figure III-1

FUNCTIONAL COST ANALYSIS
FUNDS FLOW DIAGRAM

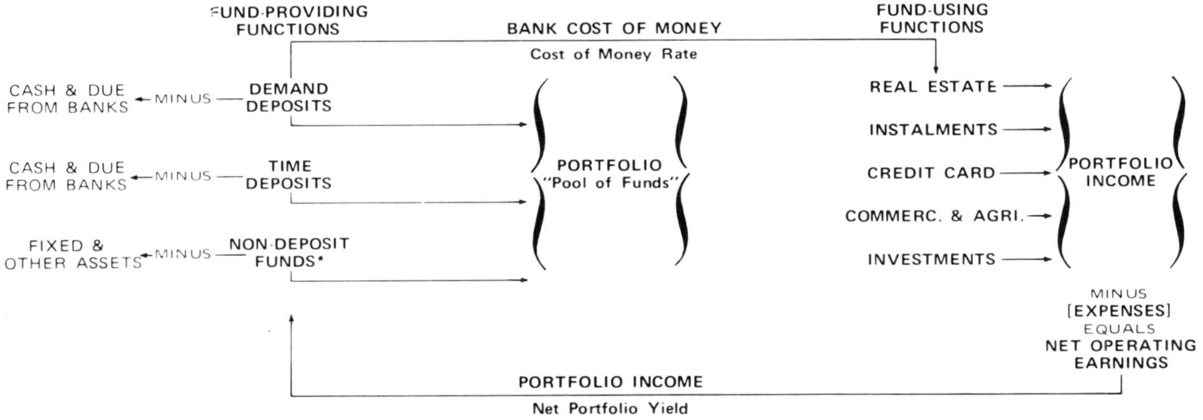

*Includes other liabilities and borrowings.

Source: Federal Reserve Bank, Functional Cost Analysis, 1975.

Data-Base

Development of comparative earnings information requires a uniform method of allocating earnings to fund-providing functions and a uniform method of applying the cost of money to fund-using functions. The Functional Cost Analysis Program is based on such a uniform method. The Program employs the "pool of funds" concept. (Refer to Figure III-1 and the following discussion.)

The "pool of funds" concept uses the same portfolio yield in calculating income for each source of funds, and charges the same "cost of money" rate to the different fund-using functions. Under this approach, pre-tax asset income is higher than shown in other analyses[59] of bank earnings, since all tax-exempt income reported in the Functional Cost Analysis Program is converted to a taxable basis. This procedure achieves interbank comparability of pre-tax earnings. Federal income taxes applicable to net current earnings (with tax exempts on a taxable basis) are calculated on the basis of current tax rates. "Below-the-line" items of income and expense are not included in the analysis because they vary greatly within a bank from year to year and among participating banks in a given year.

Information about bank assets, income, expense and item counts[60] is collected by member bankers with the guidance of uniform instructions. Although bankers must use judgments in making expense allocations, most of these judgments are required for the allocation of wages and salaries. Expenses not allocated (indirect) by the banker are allocated by the computer on the basis of "experience factors" developed from expense data of participating banks over a period of time. This technique minimizes inconsistencies of interbank comparisons. (For more details refer to Federal Reserve Bank, *Functional Cost Analysis Program - 1973 Average Banks*, pp. i-ii.)

Single Pool of Funds Concept

The underlying concept of the Functional Cost Analysis Program is the Fund Flow theory diagrammed in Figure III-1 and explained below. Three major concepts of the Functional Cost Analysis Program[61] are illustrated by the Fund Flow diagram:

1. The Pool of Funds concept of bank costing. Under this method the funds acquired through fund-providing functions are distributed to the fund-using functions.

2. The Net-Portfolio Yield, the mechanism used to credit the fund-providing functions for providing funds to the fund-using functions (loans and investments).

3. The Cost of Money Rate, the mechanism used to charge the fund-using functions for the use of the funds supplied through the demand deposit, time deposit, and non-deposit fund functions.

The Functional Cost Analysis Program is based on the bank costing concept known as the Single Pool of Funds approach. Under this approach, in contrast to other costing theories (see above discussion), specific funds provided by fund-providing functions are not matched with specific earning assets of the bank. The Pool of Funds approach accumulates all bank funds in a pool which becomes the source for bank loans and investments.

Figure III-1 depicts the pool of funds concept. The left side of the diagram represents the three fund providing functions in the cost analysis report:

1. The demand deposit function.

2. The time deposit function.

3. The non-deposit functions.

The sum of these functions constitutes the total available funds of the bank. The right side of the diagram represents the fund-using functions:

1. Real Estate function.

2. Instalment function.

3. Credit Card function.

4. Commercial and Agricultural function.

The Funds Flow diagram illustrates a second major concept of the Cost Analysis Program: the crediting of the fund-providing functions with portfolio income based on the amount of funds that are contributed (to the portfolio) by each fund-providing function. As indicated earlier, the Net Portfolio Yield is the mechanism used.

To calculate the Net Portfolio Yield,

> . . . expenses of the loan and investment functions are subtracted from gross income for these functions to obtain the net earnings for loans and investments. A percentage, which is the net portfolio yield, is then calculated by dividing the net earnings for loans and investments by the total dollar volume of loans and investments, which also equals the total dollar volume of the portfolio. By multiplying the resultant net portfolio yield times the dollar volume of funds contributed to the pool of funds of the participating bank from the demand deposit, time deposit, and non-deposit funds function, the fund-providing functions receive credit in the form of portfolio income for the contribution of funds to the earning assets of the participating bank.[62]

The third concept presented in the above illustration explains the Cost of Money Rate, the mechanism used to charge the loan and investment functions for the use of funds generated by the fund-providing functions. The rate is the internal cost of money rate based on expenses of the fund-providing functions. The rate is calculated as follows:

> . . . a separate cost of money rate is calculated for each fund-providing function . . . and a bank cost of money rate is calculated for the combined fund-providing functions. . . . The cost of money rate is a ratio used by the cost analysis program to charge the fund-using functions for use of funds loaned and invested. . . . Therefore, just as the fund-providing functions receive credit for supplying fund, the fund-using functions are charged for the use of these funds. The cost of money rate calculated by the cost analysis program is an internal cost of money rate that is unique for each bank. The cost of money rate is determined by: 1. subtracting actual income from the total expenses, resulting in the net expenses or a cost of money dollar volume, and 2. the cost of money dollar volume is divided by the corresponding asset dollar volume to obtain the cost of money rate.[63]

Structure of Reports

The annual reports published by the Federal Reserve banks are divided into three major areas:

1. a cost analysis of the overall bank

2. the actual cost analysis of the various functions

   a. Fund-providing functions
      - demand deposit function
      - time deposit function
      - non-deposit functions

b. Fund-using function
   - investment function
   - real estate, mortgage loan function
   - instalment loan function
   - credit card function
   - commercial and agricultural loan function

c. Non-fund-using functions
   - safe-deposit function
   - trust function
   - computer-service function
   - other non-banking department functions

3. the basic calculations and data adjustments that occur in the development of the reports.

Participants

All participating banks (participation is voluntary) are divided into the following three groups according to total deposits:

1. banks with total deposits of up to $50 million

2. banks with total deposits from $50 million to $200 million

3. banks with total deposits of more than $200 million.

The division of banks by deposit size permits more meaningful comparisons. For banks with total deposits of less than $50 million, the cost analysis comparisons are based on information received only from banks of similar deposit size located within the same Federal Reserve district. For banks with total deposits of $50 million to $200 million, district boundaries are sometimes crossed to obtain a sufficient number of banks of this particular deposit size to develop the comparative averages. For those banks with total deposits over $200 million, Federal Reserve district boundaries are not considered. All banks with total deposits of more than $200 million are grouped, and the number of banks required to generate the comparative averages for participating banks of this deposit size is selected from this group.

Fund Management

Allocation is at the heart of the costing process. The determination of the allocation concept is difficult and requires highly judgmental decisions because the flow of funds is difficult to trace. The method selected for allocating the cost of funds is heavily influenced by the philosophy that guides a bank in managing its funds (both sources and uses).[64]

In planning and controlling the sources and uses of funds, bank management considers the following factors:

— The nature and amount of costs and revenues associated both with obtaining and with using funds.

— Laws and regulations that establish reserve requirements and those that also influence lending practices and investment policies.

— Risks involved both in lending and investing.

— Volatility of the funds that are available to the bank for investment. One of the indicators of volatility is the turnover of funds. (Turnover is the number of times the average daily deposit balance can be divided into the total deposit flow coming into the bank in a period.)

— Liquidity of the loans and investments for which funds are used. (Liquidity is a measure of the ability of the bank to convert its loans and investments into cash, both quickly and without loss.)[65]

The Banking Industry uses most commonly the following approaches for the allocation of cost of funds to uses:

1. Single Pool of Funds concept

2. Multiple Pool of Funds concept (specific method)

3. Market-oriented Funds concept.

The Single Pool of Funds concept assumes that funds from all sources are placed into a common pool to be loaned or invested. The Multiple Pool of Funds concept, or specific method, recognizes the volatility of fund sources and the liquidity of fund uses by designating portions of each category of fund sources as being available for certain specific categories of loans and investments. Each of these concepts requires the accumulation of fund costs in cost centers (pools) for subsequent allocation to fund uses. Some of these costs are transferred to these pools from (previously compiled) cost centers.

The Market-oriented Funds concept uses current market rates (based on treasury notes or certificates of deposit) to represent the cost of the funds used. This concept is also referred to as the "incremental" method because of the assumption that the fund cost for a new loan is measured by the rate required to obtain new money in the market place. The cost of the new money is added (incremental) cost of the new loan.

Because of the difficulties inherent in designating accurately the specific fund sources used for specific categories of loans and investments, bankers often prefer to assume that all funds, regardless of their source, come from a common pool. In fact, most bankers consider the Multiple Pool of Funds concept

> . . . as being academic in character and too abstract to be of any partical application . . .[66]

Other bankers feel that the Market-oriented Funds concept is superior to the Single and Multiple Pool of Funds concepts because

> . . . these methods have limited value in communicating plans and measuring results, principally because the rates reflect historical averages, and secondarily because the calculations are complex. Even though projected into the future at increased amounts, the rates still may not reflect the realities of the market place (i.e., substantially higher rates), particularly in a tight money market.[67]

Management uses the Market-oriented Funds concept to motivate loan officers to lend funds at rates that will be profitable. Therefore, this concept is used primarily to guide day-to-day decisions. For purposes of analyzing alternatives in the planning process and aiding in longer range strategy and planning decisions, both the Single and Multiple Pool methods for allocating funds in commercial banks are used.[68]

Allocation of cost in general is a very difficult and, to a large degree, judgmental process. In the instance of the Functional Cost Analysis Program, matters are complicated by the number and diversity of organizational units (e.g., banks of differing size and philosophy). Some of these problems can never be resolved completely because arguments can be made for or against any theory advanced.

Summary

The Functional Cost Analysis Program takes a new approach to bank cost accounting. Under the Program a bank is considered a series of companies, all of which contribute to the overall results of the bank, positively and negatively. The major objective of the Functional Cost Analysis Program was not to provide sophisticated, precise cost data. The objective was the development of approximations of functional costs that would enable the participating banks to prepare year-to-year cost comparisons within the bank and with group averages of banks of similar size. This new approach taken by the Functional Cost Analysis Program ignores the traditional concept of departments and profit-centers and replaces these by functional areas, such as demand deposit, time deposit function.

Although the method of cost allocation used in the Functional Cost Analysis Program is based on some judgmental decisions on the part of bank management, the Program represents an excellent management tool for commercial banks. Bank cost accounting, and for that matter, cost accounting in general, is not an exact science. Many different systems, based on different assumptions and concepts, can be and are used today.

> There are almost as many systems as there are bank cost accountants. Because of differences in concepts, differences in degree of sophistication, and the heavy reliance on human judgment, it has been virtually impossible in the past to compare with confidence one bank's costs with those of another bank.[69]

The Functional Cost Analysis Program is the first and only program to achieve a uniform cost accounting system in the Banking Industry that permits the comparisons discussed earlier. During the late 1960's the Federal Deposit Insurance Corporation (FDIC) commissioned a study by Arthur D. Little and Company, a Cambridge, Massachusetts based consulting firm, to develop a management tool for cost analysis for its member banks. One of the conclusions reached by Arthur D. Little, after lengthy consideration, was that the Functional Cost Analysis Program was the best method available for the determination of cost data in small and medium sized commercial banks.

Critics of the Functional Cost Analysis Program frequently cite as one of the major shortcomings of the Program the possibility that the data input is compiled by lower-echelon employees. Employees who lack the knowledge and expertise required for the high-quality input information so vitally important for meaningful reports. This possibility is a serious point that warrants the closest attention of top management.

Since the individual bank's participation is voluntary on the one hand and a certain effort to compute and gather the necessary data is required on the other hand, this argument against the Functional Cost

Analysis loses much weight. Nevertheless, the quality of the Functional Cost Analysis Program and its reports depends to a great extent on the support the participating bank's management is willing to provide.

Other critics of the Program have correctly pointed to the fact that the majority of banks participating in the Program are of small and medium size. This, however, should not be construed as a weakness of the Program since the homogeneity in size enhances comparability. Furthermore, the Program was developed to provide mainly these two groups of commercial banks with a management tool in the area of cost accounting. Large banks have the means and the expertise to develop more sophisticated cost accounting systems, specifically tailored to their needs. In any event, comparisons with these "giants" of the banking industry would not be meaningful.

Applying to smaller banks some modified version of the sophisticated systems used by the large banks, as has been suggested, would not be practical. The relatively high-level knowledge of accounting that is required for the adoption of one of the more sophisticated cost concepts makes their application in small and medium sized banks all but impossible.

CHAPTER IV

METHODOLOGY

Introduction

The preceding chapter explained the Functional Cost Analysis Program and the reasons for chosing this program as data-base for this study. The purpose of this chapter is to further explain the methodology employed in the execution of the project.

The chapter begins with a brief presentation of the data-gathering device selected. Following is a listing of the purposes to be achieved through the data collected and a discussion of the rate of response to the questionnaire. Instructions to the respondents are briefly discussed, followed by sections on the development, pre-test and structure of the questionnaire. Next, the sample of commercial banks is described. The subsequent sections are devoted to explaining the development of hypothetical "long range planning scores" and the computation of actual "scores." This is followed by a detailed description of the research-partition-design, the computational procedures undertaken, the statistics used and the testing of the hypotheses. Sections on limitations of the study, an analysis of long range planning questions, and a summary conclude the chapter.

Selection of Data-Gathering Device

Subjective reports—all those measures that rely on the actor's own testimony for observing and recording behavior—probably form the largest single class of methods in the behavioral sciences for obtaining observations.[70] The three main types of these reports are: questionnaires, interviews, and tests.

Cost and time constraints, as well as the nature of the requested data, influenced the selection of the questionnaire-type report for data collection. A further reason for opting for the questionnaire is that questions used in a questionnaire, whether they be open or closed, are uniform from respondent to respondent, because they are written on paper. Questions can vary in their effects, however, because of misreadings or unfamiliarity with style of language.[71]

All but two questions used in this project are closed. Respondents were given the opportunity to make additional comments on any question included in the questionnaire. For further details in the advantages and disadvantages of questionnaires as data-collection tools, refer to Runkel and McGrath[72] or any standard textbook.

Purpose of the Questionnaire

The main goals of this research are the determination of the extent to which commercial banks are engaging in long range planning and the impact of long range planning on profit- and growth-trends in commercial banks. A thorough review of the literature in the area of planning in banks, both in Europe and the United States, revealed a general paucity of research. A questionnaire was designed to permit the collection of data for reporting and measuring in order to achieve the following specific objectives:

1. determine the extent to which the responding banks engage in long range planning activities,
2. determine the extent to which commercial banks are using long range planning techniques and what these techniques are,
3. develop profiles of commercial banks by size, community, economic environment, etc., and of the long range planning efforts undertaken,
4. classify responding banks by extent of planning activities,
5. classify responding banks by size,
6. determine the change in growth and profit trends of responding banks.

Criteria for Execution of Data-Building Phase

An adequate response rate is one of the important conditions affecting the success and validity of a research project which depends on a survey. In an effort to achieve an adequate rate of response to the questionnaire, the following steps were taken:

1. Guarantee confidentiality of data and anonymity of respondents. The review of the literature, and the many discussions that took place with bankers during the developmental stages of the questionnaire revealed that potential participants in the research project would be very much concerned about the confidentiality of any data they might supply. To put these concerns to rest, respondents were

assured of the confidentiality of any data and their responses at the beginning of the questionnaire. Respondents were also advised that no bank would be singled out in the analysis and that all data would be used in aggregation only.

2. Promise the sharing of results of the research to compensate respondents for their investment in time.

3. Obtain sponsorship of the Banking industry. Proper sponsorship of this project was thought to be another prime ingredient for success. A cover letter, over the signature of the President of the Bank Administration Institute, was mailed with the questionnaire to all banks selected for the project. Commercial banks are literally deluged by requests for information, not only by researchers and financial analysts, but also, and more importantly, by State and Federal Regulatory Agencies. While banks can ignore the requests of the first group, they have to comply with the "requests" of the second group.

4. Hold required completion time to a minimum.

5. Use commonly understood terminology.

6. Make answers as simple as possible, e.g., use check-marks rather than verbal answers.

7. Hold the number of essay-type answers required to a minimum, but provide the opportunity for airing of strong convictions and suggestions. This allows feedback to confirm validity of questions.

8. Mimeograph rather than print questionnaire to distinguish it from most "information-requests" that banks receive from a variety of regulatory agencies.

9. Arrange questions in such a manner that interest in questionnaire is stimulated and that the most time-consuming questions appear at the end of the questionnaire. Respondents are not expected to abandon the project when only one or two more questions, though a little more time consuming, remain to be answered.

10. To keep number of questions low, use sub-questions. Evans (1977)[73] subdivided a total of 120 questions into sections. The overall rate of response of 26% achieved in his study was attributed, at least in part, to this procedure.

11. Organize questionnaire through format adopted and typing style selected in such a way as to hold the number of pages to a minimum.

Instructions to the Respondents

The cover letter mailed together with the questionnaire informed the banks that the data and information requested were for dissertation research and that the Bank Administration Institute was supporting the project because the results would be of interest to the industry. The Institute advised participants that it recommended cooperation in the study. A copy of the cover letter is included in Appendix A.

Instructions for the submission of all data were an integral part of the questionnaire and cover letter. The responding banks were asked to reply directly to the author of the research by using the self-addressed envelope provided.

Development of the Questionnaire

The questionnaire used in the study was developed in several steps. A copy of the questionnaire is included in Appendix A.

First, a thorough review of the planning literature was conducted and questionnaires used in bank-related studies were examined with reference to the objectives of this research project. This initial input to the formulation of the questionnaire was discussed with top managers and officials of local, national, and international banks. At the same time researchers specializing in banking were consulted through personal interviews.

A preliminary draft of the questionnaire, which incorporated all recommendations and suggestions received during the initial phase, was discussed with officials of the Bank Administration Institute in Park Ridge, Illinois on two occasions, in late 1975 and early 1976. Valuable feedback was also received from members of the research department of the Federal Reserve Bank of Chicago in early 1976.

During August 1975 and January 1976, extensive discussions were held with representatives of several German banks (leaders in planning research in Germany) in Munich and Dillingen an der Donau. These discussions were extremely helpful since they provided a different point of view and also gave access to important information and literature pertaining to the topic of the research.

Interviews with the controller of a large bank in Lexington, Kentucky, and with several executives of some of the nations largest

Chicago-based banks provided valuable information. Individuals contacted were responsible for their bank's planning activities.

Pre-Test of the Questionnaire

A revised draft of the questionnaire was pre-tested in personal interviews at several banks in Chicago, ranging in size from $30 million to $15 billion in total deposits. During the testing the interviewer briefly explained the purpose of the research to the executive and then asked for the completion of the questionnaire. The interviewees were encouraged to ask for clarifications when needed. Recommendations and observations obtained from this pre-test were considered in preparing the final version of the questionnaire.

Structure of the Questionnaire

To facilitate the achievement of the goals and objectives stated previously, the questionnaire was organized in the following sections:

1. Instructions to the respondents.
2. Assurance of confidentiality.
3. Demographical data (questions 1 - 7).
4. Information related to planning activities (questions 8 - 25).
5. Functional Cost Analysis data for average deposits and Net Yield after Cost of Cash.

Questions 1 through 7 were included in the questionnaire to collect data regarding the bank's charter, number of branches, size of trading area, profile of service area, dependence on locally dominant industry, length of service of chief-executive, and share of local banking market. Information collected through questions in this section was used in the development of "bank-profiles" in terms of long range planning activities. For a detailed discussion, refer to the section on "Cross-tabulations" below.

Questions 8 through 25 ask for specific information regarding planning practices and the extent of use of these practices. These questions have a two-fold purpose:

1. provide the basis for the computation of the long range planning "score" used to partition the responding banks into three groups

according to the extent to which they engage in long range planning;

2. provide information to determine the extent to which long range planning is used in commercial banks (development of bank-profiles referred to above).

Questions 8 through 25 are the results of an extensive review of the planning literature and numerous discussions, interviews, and a pre-test of the questionnaire. The definition of long range planning in commercial banks (refer to above section on definitions) was the fulcrum of this part of the questionnaire. Underlying criteria for the formulation of the questions were the completeness of the planning process, time horizon employed, frequency of revisions and up-date of plans, degree of detail, and degree of flexibility. All long range planning questions included in the questionnaire were linked to the definition of long range planning in commercial banks. Refer to Appendix D for a complete analysis.

The purpose of the last question, number 26, was to obtain financial data regarding average deposits and net yield after cost of cash (as defined and used in the annual Functional Cost Analysis reports). The data, requested for the years 1970 through 1974, are based on the Functional Cost Analysis Program to assure comparability from year to year within a bank and among participating banks. For a detailed discussion refer to Chapter III.

The time frame for the study was limited to the period 1970 through 1974 for the following reasons:

1. to eliminate the effect of regulatory reporting requirement changes which took place in 1969 and 1975;

2. to determine the extent to which long range planning is used as a management tool today, as compared to the extent to which it was used during the mid-1960's when a new awareness of its value to commercial banks developed.[74]

3. to obtain a sufficiently large sample of commercial banks (banks that participated without interruption in the Functional Cost Analysis Program for the period under review). The longer the time period under review, the more reduced is the list of continuous participants in the program. Blum and Vasicek (1971),[75] in their research on "efficient markets," experienced "losses" of potential sample firms of up to 75% when considering

time periods of 7 years and more. As data-bank they used the Compustat tape of New York Stock Exchange-traded companies.

Average deposits for the year 1970 were used to classify the responding banks into size classes as follows:

Bank size A: Banks with total average deposits of more than $200 million;

Bank size B: Banks with total average deposits from $50 million to $200 million;

Bank size C: Banks with total average deposits of up to $50 million.

These categories follow the classification system used by the Federal Reserve Bank in the Cost Analysis Program.

Average deposits for the years 1970 through 1974 were also used as surrogates for the computation of growth trends. (Refer to detailed discussion below.) "Memo-Net Yields after Cost of Cash" (for the same years) were used for the computation of profit trends for all responding banks. (Refer to further discussion below.)

The last page of the questionnaire provided space for specific comments on question 20j (use of the computer in long range planning) and question 20k (use of econometric models in long range planning). Respondents were encouraged to make comments in general on the same page.

Sample of Commercial Banks

Sample Size

An important question as far as sample design is concerned is the determination of an appropriate sample size. If the sample is larger than necessary, resources are wasted; if the sample is smaller than required, the objectives of the analysis may not be achieved.

The population for this project is comprised of all commercial banks in the United States. Because of cost and time constraints, the study is limited to banks which are members of one Federal Reserve district. A further consideration for the selection of only one of the twelve districts was the significant differences that exist in banking resources and volume of transactions handled.[76] A further requirement for inclusion in the project was Functional Cost Analysis participation.

This study, therefore, is concerned only with those commercial banks that are members of the 7th Federal Reserve district and participants in the Functional Cost Analysis Program, since data sufficient for a complete study are available only for those banks.

Mailing

In June 1976 the questionnaire, together with the cover letter from the Bank Administration Institute, was mailed to 144 commercial banks, all members of the 7th Federal Reserve district.[77] One hundred forty one of the banks that received the questionnaire had participated in the Functional Cost Analysis Program of the Federal Reserve Bank System from 1970 through 1974. These 141 banks were identified on lists of Functional Cost Analysis participants supplied by the Federal Reserve Bank of Chicago.

To insure proper routing of the questionnaire within each bank and thus increase the rate of response and also improve the quality of the data supplied, the questionnaires were addressed and mailed to senior officials and executives of the 144 banks. Names and current addresses of these individuals were obtained from Rand McNally's International Bankers Directory, Final 1975 Edition.

Responses

Of the 144 questionnaires mailed, 77 were returned by the respondents, representing a response rate of 53%. Seventy-six percent of the returned questionnaires were complete as to both parts, long range planning questions and data request. Twenty-four percent of the returned questionnaires were incomplete with regard to the data requested in question No. 26. These questionnaires, therefore, were excluded from the analysis of growth and profit trends in relation to long range planning.

The 18 questionnaires which did not include answers to question No. 26 were tested to determine whether they were different from the remaining questionnaires. The t-test of the mean LRP-Scores at the 1% level revealed no statistically significant difference.

Hypothetical Long Range Planning Score

The purpose of the following section is to explain the reasons and procedures used in computing "long range planning scores." As indicated earlier, questions 8 through 25 were designed to report and measure the extent to which commerical banks (included in the study) engage in long range planning activities. The research design adopted for this project required the partitioning of all banks on two planes:

1. vertically, according to size (as determined by average deposits during 1970);
2. horizontally, according to the extent of long range planning undertaken (refer to research-partition-design in Figure IV-1 in this chapter).

In the absence of a single criterion for the measurement of the extent of long range planning, questions 8 through 25 were included in the questionnaire to permit the development of a measurement surrogate. There are 55 questions and subquestions pertaining to the extent of long range planning. All are yes-no questions and each is considered to be of equal importance. In computing "scores" for each respondent, each *yes* answer will be awarded with one point, each *no* answer (or *not applicable*) will be awarded with zero points. The highest "score" then that a bank could achieve (all 55 questions are answered with *yes*) would be 55, the lowest possible "score" would be zero (that is, all 55 questions are answered with *no* or *not applicable*).

Before the mailing of the questionnaire, a "hypothetical long range planning score" was developed for a "typical bank" of each bank size. Discussions with bankers, Federal Reserve Bank officers, controllers, Bank Administration Institute officials, and others indicated that the assumed respondents' scores might lead to the following classification system:

Extent of long range planning	Score
High	38 to 55
Moderate	16 to 37
Low	0 to 15

Hypothetical scores to illustrate the above are in Appendix C.

Actual Long Range Planning Score

Upon receipt of the completed questionnaires the 55 long range planning questions, referred to above, served as the basis for the computation of the actual long range planning score for each responding bank. A description of the computation of the actual scores follows.

For purposes of statistical analysis, it was desirable to divide the banks, according to the extent of long range planning, into three approximately equal groups. The mean long range planning score and its standard deviation were chosen as the most appropriate mechanism to achieve this partition.

The "mean score" for all responding banks was computed as follows:

$$\overline{X} = \frac{\sum_{i=1}^{n} x_i}{n}$$

where x_i = the ith bank's long range planning score,
n = number of banks responding,
$\overline{X}$ = mean long range planning score.

The computed mean long range planning score for all responding banks was 25.584, with a standard deviation of 13.001. This mean plus and minus 1/2 standard deviation (25.584 ± 6.50) was used to determine three long range planning categories as follows: All banks whose scores fell within 1/2 standard deviation above or below the mean were classified as moderate long range planning banks; banks whose scores were higher than the mean plus 1/2 standard deviation were considered high long range planning banks; while banks whose scores were lower than the mean minus 1/2 standard deviation, were considered low long range planning banks. The resulting categories are as follows:

Extent of long range planning	Long range planning score	
High	33-55	(25.584 + 6.5)
Moderate	19-32	(25.584 ± 6.5)
Low	0-18	(25.584 − 6.5)

Comparing the "hypothetical scores" computed before the mailing of the questionnaire with the actual results reveals a very high correlation between the two measures. This high correlation lends credence to the preliminary computation of long range planning scores and also presents additional evidence for the validity of the classification method chosen.

Research - Partition - Design

As explained earlier, the data analysis consists of two parts:

1. the impact of long range planning activities on profit and growth trends;
2. the determination of the extent to which long range planning is used by commercial banks.

The following sections describe the procedures employed in the analysis of the goal referred to under No. 1 above.

Average deposits for 1970 and the above-developed long range planning score were used to classify the responding banks into mutually exclusive subgroups (partitions). Refer to Figure IV-1.

Data Arrangement and Computations

A series of hypotheses (see below) is formulated to determine the following: Can the extent of long range planning undertaken by banks be linked with bank size? Are profits and growth affected by bank size, or by extent of long range planning activities undertaken? How do differing degrees of long range planning activities affect profits and growth of banks of the same size?

The following procedures were used[78] to arrange the data in such a manner as to permit the desired testing of hypotheses. A description of the sequence of steps taken follows a detailed listing of all hypotheses.

Hypotheses

To achieve the above stated goals, the following specific hypotheses will be tested:

H_{1A}: Banks of size ‘A’ do not engage in significantly more Long Range Planning (LRP) than do banks of size ‘B’.

H_{1B}: Banks of size ‘B’ do not engage in significantly more LRP than do banks of size ‘C’.

H_{2A}: Banks of size ‘A’ do not experience significantly higher percentage changes in growth than do banks of size ‘B’.

Figure IV-1

Research-Partition-Design

Partition No. 1 Banks with deposits of $200 million or more and a long range planning score of at least 33 points	Partition No. 2 Banks with deposits of $200 million or more and a long range planning score of at least 19 but less than 33 points	Partition No. 3 Banks with deposits of $200 million or more and a long range planning score of less than 19 points
Partition No. 4 Banks with deposits of at least $50 million but less than $200 million and a long range planning score of at least 33 points	Partition No. 5 Banks with deposits of at least $50 million but less than $200 million and a long range planning score of at least 19 points but less than 33 points	Partition No. 6 Banks with deposits of at least $50 million but less than $200 million and a long range planning score of less than 19 points
Partition No. 7 Banks with deposits of less than $50 million and a long range planning score of at least 33 points	Partition No. 8 Banks with deposits of less than $50 million and a long range planning score of at least 19 but but less than 33 points	Partition No. 9 Banks with deposits of less than $50 million and a long range planning score of less than 19 points

H_{2B}: Banks of size 'B' do not experience significantly higher percentage changes in growth than do banks of size 'C'.

H_{3A}: Banks of size 'A' do not experience significantly higher percentage changes in profit than do banks of size 'B'.

H_{3B}: Banks of size 'B' do not experience significantly higher percentage changes in profit than do banks of size 'C'.

H_{4A}: Banks engaging to a high degree in LRP do not experience significantly higher changes in growth than do banks engaging to a moderate degree in LRP.

H_{4B}: Banks engaging to a moderate degree in LRP do not experience significantly higher changes in growth than do banks engaging to a low degree in LRP.

H_{5A}: Banks engaging to a high degree in LRP do not experience significantly higher changes in profit than do banks engaging to a moderate degree in LRP.

H_{5B}: Banks engaging to a moderate degree in LRP do not experience significantly higher changes in profit than do banks engaging to a moderate degree in LRP.

H_{6A}: Banks in cell No. 1 do not experience significantly different percentage changes in growth than do banks in cell No. 4.

H_{6B}: Banks in cell No. 4 do not experience significantly different percentage changes in growth than do banks in cell No. 7.

H_{7A}: Banks in cell No. 1 do not experience significantly different percentage changes in profit than do banks in cell No. 4.

H_{7B}: Banks in cell No. 4 do not experience significantly different percentage changes in profit than do banks in cell No. 7.

H_{8A}: Banks in cell No. 2 do not experience significantly different percentage changes in growth than do banks in cell No. 5.

H_{8B}: Banks in cell No. 5 do not experience significantly different percentage changes in growth than do banks in cell No. 8.

H_{9A}: Banks in cell No. 2 do not experience significantly different percentage changes in profit than do banks in cell No. 5.

H_{9B}: Banks in cell No. 5 do not experience significantly different percentage changes in profit than do banks in cell No. 8.

H_{10A}: Banks in cell No. 3 do not experience significantly different percentage changes in growth than do banks in cell No. 6.

H_{10B}: Banks in cell No. 6 do not experience significantly different percentage changes in growth than do banks in cell No. 9.

H_{11A}: Banks in cell No. 3 do not experience significantly different percentage changes in profit than do banks in cell No. 6.

H_{11B}: Banks in cell No. 6 do not experience significantly different percentage changes in profit than do banks in cell No. 9.

H_{12A}: Banks of size 'A' engaging to a high degree in LRP (banks in cell No. 1) do not experience significantly different percentage changes in growth than do banks of size 'A' engaging to a moderate degree in LRP (banks in cell No. 2).

H_{12B}: Banks in cell No. 2 do not experience significantly different percentage changes in growth than do banks in cell No. 3.

H_{13A}: Banks in cell No. 1 do not experience significantly different percentage changes in profit than do banks in cell No. 2.

H_{13B}: Banks in cell No. 2 do not experience significantly different percentage changes in profit than do banks in cell No. 3.

H_{14A}: Banks in cell No. 4 do not experience significantly different percentage changes in growth than do banks in cell No. 5.

H_{14B}: Banks in cell No. 5 do not experience significantly different percentage changes in growth than do banks in cell No. 6.

H_{15A}: Banks in cell No. 4 do not experience significantly different percentage changes in profit than do banks in cell No. 5.

H_{15B}: Banks in cell No. 5 do not experience significantly different percentage changes in profit than do banks in cell No. 6.

H_{16A}: Banks in cell No. 7 do not experience significantly different percentage changes in growth than do banks in cell No. 8.

H_{16B}: Banks in cell No. 8 do not experience significantly different percentage changes in growth than do banks in cell No. 9.

H_{17A}: Banks in cell No. 7 do not experience significantly different percentage changes in profit than do banks in cell No. 8.

H_{17B}: Banks in cell No. 8 do not experience significantly different percentage changes in profit than do banks in cell No. 9.

A detailed discussion of the statistical procedures applied in the testing of the hypotheses is included in this chapter. The results of the tests are presented in Chapter V. Inferences and conclusions are summarized in Chapter VI.

For subsequent discussions and references the above listed hypotheses are presented in the following section in graphic form. All graphs follow the same pattern. Horizontally the graphs are divided according to the extent of long range planning undertaken by the bank (high, moderate, low) and vertically they are classified according to bank size (Class A = large, class B = medium, class C = small).

Figure IV-2

Hypotheses

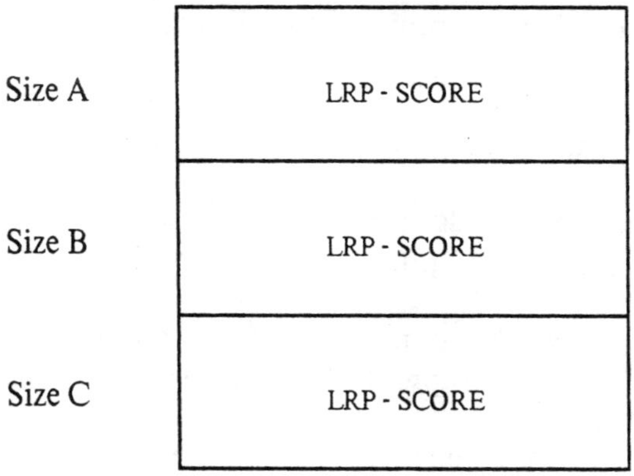

$H_{1A,B}$

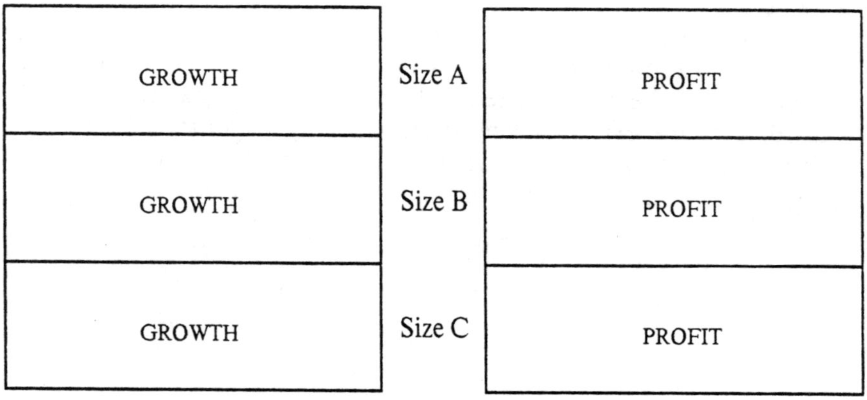

$H_{2A,B}$ $H_{3A,B}$

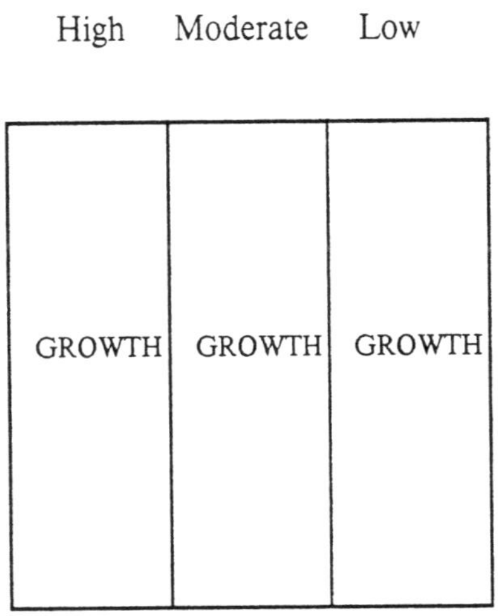

$H_{4A,B}$

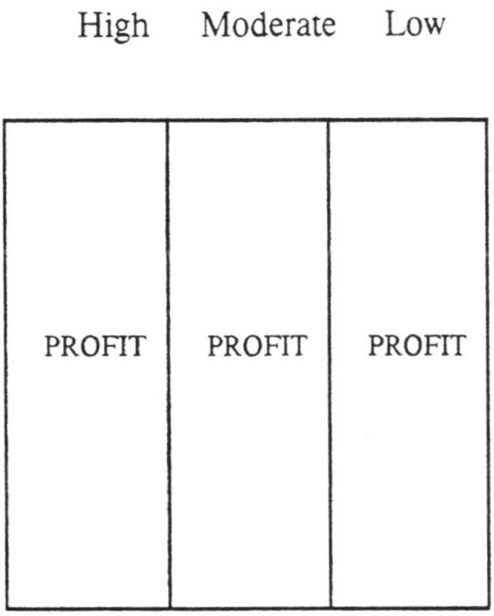

$H_{5A,B}$

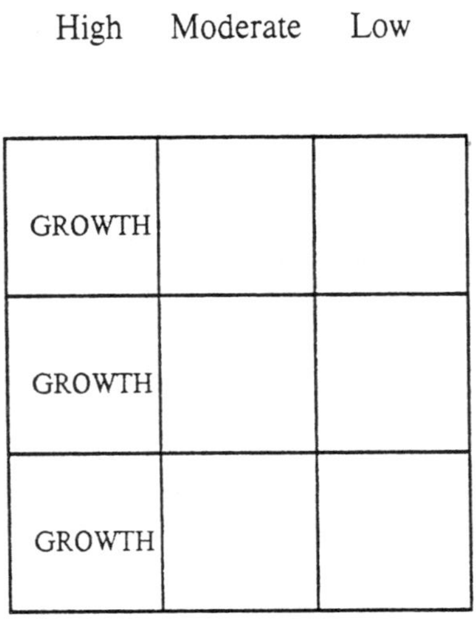

$H_{6A,B}$

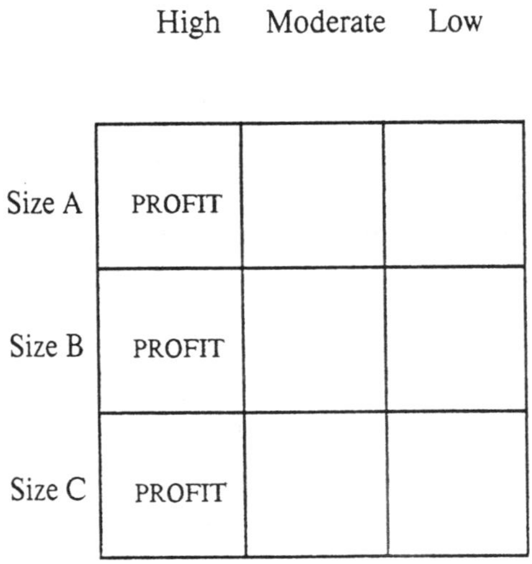

$H_{7A,B}$

	High	Moderate	Low
Size A		GROWTH	
Size B		GROWTH	
Size C		GROWTH	

$H_{8A,B}$

	High	Moderate	Low
Size A		PROFIT	
Size B		PROFIT	
Size C		PROFIT	

$H_{9A,B}$

	High	Moderate	Low
Size A			GROWTH
Size B			GROWTH
Size C			GROWTH

$H_{10A,B}$

	High	Moderate	Low
Size A			PROFIT
Size B			PROFIT
Size C			PROFIT

$H_{11A,B}$

	High	Moderate	Low
Size A	GROWTH	GROWTH	GROWTH
Size B			
Size C			

$H_{12A,B}$

	High	Moderate	Low
Size A	PROFIT	PROFIT	PROFIT
Size B			
Size C			

$H_{13A,B}$

	High	Moderate	Low
Size A			
Size B	GROWTH	GROWTH	GROWTH
Size C			

$H_{14A,B}$

	High	Moderate	Low
Size A			
Size B	PROFIT	PROFIT	PROFIT
Size C			

$H_{15A,B}$

	High	Moderate	Low
Size A			
Size B			
Size C	GROWTH	GROWTH	GROWTH

$H_{16A,B}$

	High	Moderate	Low
Size A			
Size B			
Size C	PROFIT	PROFIT	PROFIT

$H_{17A,B}$

Step No. 1: Geometric Mean-Growth for all Banks[79]

For each bank the Geometric Mean (G) of changes in deposits for the period of 1970 to 1974 was computed as follows:

$$G = \sqrt[n]{x_1 \cdot x_2 \cdot \ldots x_n}$$

where x_1 = average deposits in 1970 for each respondent, x_2 = average deposits in 1971 for each respondent, etc. The Geometric Mean was computed for all banks that returned a fully completed questionnaire (77 banks answered questions 1 through 25, while 59 banks answered questions 1 through 26). Refer to Appendix E for a more detailed discussion of the Geometric Mean.

Step No. 2: Geometric Mean-Profit for all Banks[80]

For each bank the Geometric Mean of changes in "Net Yield for Portfolio, Loans and Investments" was computed. The procedure is identical to the procedure used in step No. 1.

Step No. 3: Mean LRP-Score for Banks of Size A, B, C

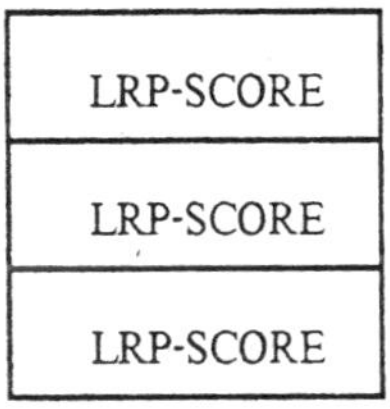

Using the previously determined "long range planning score" for each bank, the Arithmetic Mean long range planning score for all banks of size A (banks with $200 million or more in average deposits in 1970 - partitions No. 1, No. 2, and No. 3) was computed. The procedure is repeated for all banks of size B (banks with at least $50 million but less than $200 million in average deposits in 1970 - partitions No. 4, No. 5, and No. 6), and all banks of size C (banks with less than $50 million in average deposits in 1970 - partitions No. 7, No. 8, and No. 9).

The formula used for the computation of the Arithmetic Mean is as follows:

$$\overline{X} = \frac{\sum_{i}^{n} x}{n}$$

where $\overline{X}$ = arithmetic mean

x_i = the ith bank's long range planning score

n = the number of banks included in the computation of the mean.

Step No. 4: Mean Growth-Change for Banks of Size A, B, C

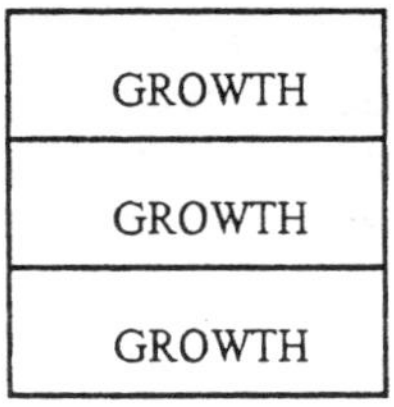

The Geometric Means of changes in deposits (surrogates for growth), computed under step No. 1 for each bank, served as the basis for the computation of the Arithmetic Mean for all banks of size A. The procedure was repeated for all banks of sizes B and C.

Step No. 5: Mean Profit-Change for Banks of Size A, B, C

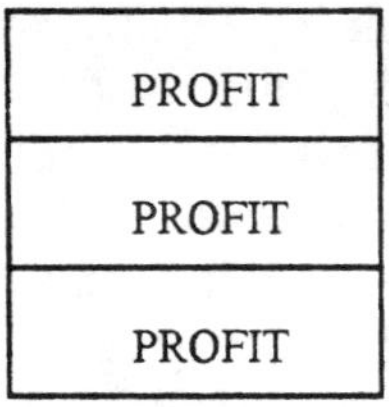

The Geometric Means of changes in "Net Yield for Portfolio, Loans and Investments" (surrogate for profit), computed for each bank under step No. 2, served as the basis for the calculation of the Arithmetic Mean for all banks of size A (banks with $200 million or more in average deposits—partitions No. 1, No. 2, or No. 3). The procedure was repeated for banks of sizes B and C.

Step No. 6: Mean Growth-Change for Banks According to LRP

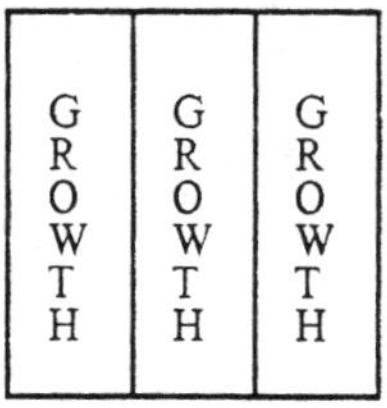

Using the Geometric Means of changes in deposits, computed for each bank under step No. 1, the Arithmetic Mean for all banks engaging to a high degree in long range planning (partitions No. 1, No. 4, and No. 7) was determined. The procedure is repeated to determine the Arithmetic Mean of changes in deposits for all banks engaging to a moderate degree in long range planning (partitions No. 2, No. 5, and No. 8) and all banks engaging to a low degree in long range planning (partitions No. 3, No. 6, and No. 9).

Step No. 7: Mean Profit-Change for Banks According to LRP

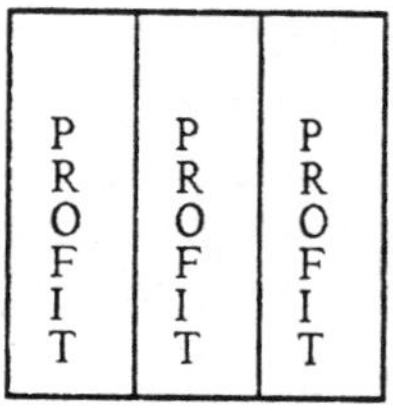

Using the Geometric Means of changes in "Net Yield for portfolio, Loans and Investments," computed for each bank under step No. 2, the Arithmetic Mean for all banks engaging to a high degree in long range planning (partitions No. 1, No. 4, and No. 7) was determined. The procedure was repeated for all banks engaging to a moderate degree in long range planning (partitions No. 2, No. 5, and No. 8) and all banks engaging to a low degree in long range planning (partitions No. 3, No. 6, and No. 9).

Step No. 8: Mean Growth-Change for Banks (Partitions 1, 4, 7)

GRO		
GRO		
GRO		

Using the Geometric Means of changes in deposits, computed for each bank under step No. 1, the Arithmetic Mean for all banks in partition No. 1 was determined. The procedure was repeated to determine the Arithmetic Mean for banks in partitions No. 4 and No. 7.

Step No. 9: Mean Profit-Change for Banks (Partitions 1, 4, 7)

PRO		
PRO		
PRO		

Using the Geometric Means of changes in "Net Yield for portfolio, Loans and Investments," computed under step No. 2 for each bank, the Arithmetic Mean for all banks in partition No. 1 was determined. The procedure was repeated to determine the Arithmetic Mean for banks in partitions No. 4 and No. 7.

Step No. 10: Mean Growth-Change for Banks (Partitions 2, 5, 8)

	GRO	
	GRO	
	GRO	

Using the Geometric Means of changes in deposits, computed for each bank under step No. 1, the Arithmetic Mean for all banks in partition No. 2 was determined. The procedure was repeated to determine the Arithmetic Mean for banks in partitions No. 5 and No. 8.

Step No. 11: Mean Profit-Change for Banks (Partitions 2, 5, 8)

	PRO	
	PRO	
	PRO	

Using the Geometric Means of changes in "Net Yield . . . ," computed under step No. 2 for each bank, the Arithmetic Mean for all banks in partition No. 2 was determined. The procedure was repeated to determine the Arithmetic Mean for banks in partitions No. 5 and No. 8.

Step No. 12: Mean Growth-Change for Banks (Partitions 3, 6, 9)

		GRO
		GRO
		GRO

Using the Geometric Means of changes in deposits, computed for each bank under step No. 1, the Arithmetic Mean for all banks in partition No. 3 was determined. The procedure was repeated to determine the Arithmetic Mean for banks in partitions No. 6 and No. 9.

Step No. 13: Mean Profit-Change for Banks (Partitions 3, 6, 9)

		PRO
		PRO
		PRO

Using the Geometric Means of changes in "Net Yield . . . ," computed under step No. 2 for each bank, the Arithmetic Mean for all banks in partition No. 3 was determined. The procedure was repeated to determine the Arithmetic Mean for banks in partitions No. 6 and No. 9.

Step No. 14: Mean Growth-Change for Banks (Partitions 1, 2, 3)

GRO	GRO	GRO

Using the Geometric Means of changes in deposits, computed for each bank under step No. 1, the Arithmetic Mean for all banks in partition No. 1 was determined. The procedure was repeated to determine the Arithmetic Mean for banks in partitions No. 2 and No. 3.

Step No. 15: Mean Profit-Change for Banks (Partitions 1, 2, 3)

PRO	PRO	PRO

Using the Geometric Means of changes in "Net Yield . . . ," computed under step No. 2 for each bank, the Arithmetic Mean for all banks in partition No. 1 was determined. The procedure was repeated to determine the Arithmetic Mean for banks in partitions No. 2 and No. 3.

Step No. 16: Mean Growth-Change for Banks (Partitions 4, 5, 6)

GRO	GRO	GRO

Using the Geometric Means of changes in deposits, computed for each bank under step No. 1, the Arithmetic Mean for all banks in partition No. 4 was determined. The procedure was repeated to determine the Arithmetic Mean for banks in partitions No. 5 and No. 6.

Step No. 17: Mean Profit-Change for Banks (Partitions 4, 5, 6)

PRO	PRO	PRO

Using the Geometric Means of changes in "Net Yield . . . ," computed under step No. 2 for each bank, the Arithmetic Mean for all banks in partition No. 4 was determined. The procedure was repeated to determine the Arithmetic Mean for banks in partitions No. 5 and No. 6.

Step No. 18: Mean Growth-Change for Banks (Partitions 7, 8, 9)

GRO	GRO	GRO

Using the Geometric Means of changes in deposits, computed for each bank under step No. 1, the Arithmetic Mean for all banks in partition No. 7 was determined. The procedure was repeated to determine the Arithmetic Mean for banks in partitions No. 8 and No. 9.

Step No. 19: Mean Profit-Change for Banks (Partitions 7, 8, 9)

PRO	PRO	PRO

Using the Geometric Means of changes in "Net Yield . . . ," computed under step No. 2 for each bank, the Arithmetic Mean for all banks in partition No. 7 was determined. The procedure was repeated to determine the Arithmetic Mean for banks in partitions No. 8 and No. 9.

Statistics Employed to Test the Hypotheses

When alternative statistical tests are available for a research design, a rationale for choosing among them must be provided. One important criterion used to decide which techniques to adopt is the power of the statistical test.[81] The most powerful tests are those which have the strongest or most extensive assumptions. Furthermore, a statistical test is a good one if it has a small probability of rejecting H_0 when H_0 is true, but a large probability of rejecting H_0 when H_0 is false.[82]

The F-test, a parametric test, has a variety of strong assumptions underlying its use. When those assumptions are valid, the F-test will be more powerful than any other in rejecting H_0 when it is false.

The conditions which must be satisfied for the F-test to be a powerful test[83] are as follows:

1. The observations must be drawn from normally distributed populations.
2. The observations must be independent. That is, the selection of any one case from the population, for inclusion in the sample, must not bias the chances of any other case for inclusion, and the score which is assigned to any case must not bias the score which is assigned to any other case.
3. These populations must have the same variance (or, in special cases, they must have a known ratio of variances).
4. The variables involved must have been measured in at least an interval scale, so that it is possible to use the operations of arithmetic (adding, dividing, finding means, etc.) on the scores.
5. The means of these normal and homoscedastic populations must be linear combinations of effects due to columns and/or rows. That is, the effects must be additive.

All of the above conditions (except No. 4, which states the measurement requirement) are elements of the parametric statistical model. With the possible exception of the assumption of homoscedasticity (equal variances), these conditions are ordinarily not tested in the course of the performance of a statistical analysis. Rather, they are presumptions which are accepted, and their truth or falsity determines the meaningfulness of the probability statement arrived at by the parametric test . . .

Siegel goes on and states:

When we have reason to believe that these conditions are met in the data under analysis, then we should certainly choose a parametric statistical test, such as the t- or F-test, for analyzing those data. Such a choice is optimum because the parametric test will be most powerful for rejecting H_0 when it should be rejected.

Since there were no indications that the above conditions were not met, the F-test was used in the analysis of the data in this study. The actual computations required for the testing of the hypotheses are explained below. (Some calculations were explained earlier.)

Testing of the Hypotheses

The hypotheses developed earlier (refer to listing above) were tested as follows:

Step No. 20: Test for H_{1A} and H_{1B}

LRP-SCORE
LRP-SCORE
LRP-SCORE

To test hypotheses H_{1A} and H_{1B}, the long range planning score means, computed under Step No. 3 for each bank size category, were examined for statistically significant differences at the 5% and 10% level of significance by using the F-test.

Step No. 21: Test for H_{2A} and H_{2B}

GROWTH
GROWTH
GROWTH

To test hypotheses H_{2A} and H_{2B}, the Arithmetic Means for each bank size category (computed under step No. 4) were examined for significant statistical differences at the 5% and 10% level of significance by using the F-test.

Step No. 22: Test for H_{3A} and H_{3B}

PROFIT
PROFIT
PROFIT

To test hypotheses H_{3A} and H_{3B}, the Arithmetic Means for each bank size category (computed under Step No. 5) were examined for statistically significant differences at the 5% and 10% level of significance by using the F-test.

Step No. 23: Test for H_{4A} and H_{4B}

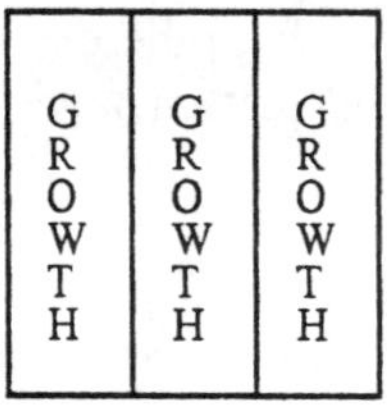

To test Hypotheses H_{4A} and H_{4B}, the Arithmetic Means for each long range planning category (computed under step No. 6) were examined for statistically significant differences at the 5% and 10% level of significance by using the F-test.

Step No. 24: Test for H_{5A} and H_{5B}

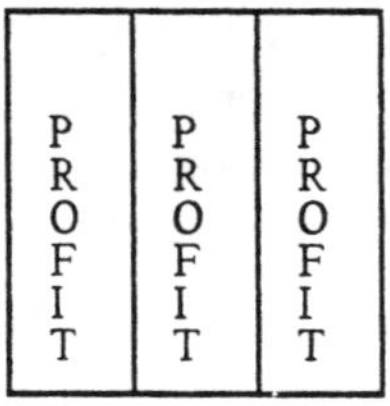

To test hypotheses H_{5A} and H_{5B}, the Arithmetic Means for each long range planning category (computed under Step No. 7) were examined for statistically significant differences at the 5% and 10% level of significance by using the F-test.

Step No. 25: Test for H_{6A} and H_{6B}

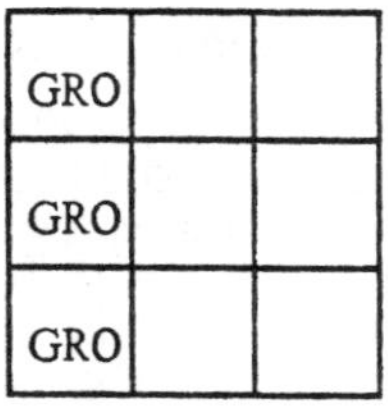

To test hypotheses H_{6A} and H_{6B}, the Arithmetic Means for partitions No. 1, No. 4, and No. 7 (computed under step No. 8) were examined for statistically significant differences at the 5% and 10% level of significance by using the F-test.

Step No. 26: Test for H_{7A} and H_{7B}

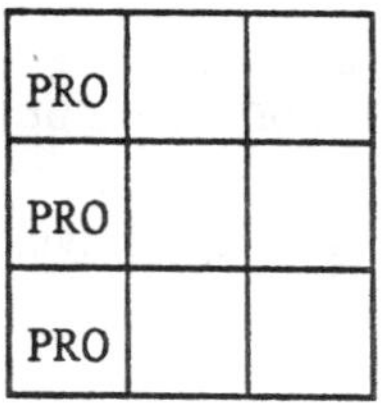

To test hypotheses H_{7A} and H_{7B}, the Arithmetic Means for partitions No. 1, No. 4, and No. 7 (computed under step No. 9) were examined for statistically significant differences at the 5% and 10% level of significance by using the F-test.

Step No. 27: Test for H_{8A} and H_{8B}

	GRO	
	GRO	
	GRO	

To test hypotheses H_{8A} and H_{8B}, the Arithmetic Means for partitions No. 2, No. 5, and No. 8 (computed under Step No. 10) were examined for statistically significant differences at the 5% and 10% level of significance by using the F-test.

Step No. 28: Test for H_{9A} and H_{9B}

	PRO	
	PRO	
	PRO	

To test hypotheses H_{9A} and H_{9B}, the Arithmetic Means for partitions No. 2, No. 5, and No. 8 (computed under step No. 11) were examined for statistically significant differences at the 5% and 10% level of significance by using the F-test.

Step No. 29: Test for H_{10A} and H_{10B}

		GRO
		GRO
		GRO

To test hypotheses H_{10A} and H_{10B}, the Arithmetic Means for partitions No. 3, No. 6, and No. 9 (computed under step No. 12) were examined for statistically significant differences at the 5% and 10% level of significance by using the F-test.

Step No. 30 Test for H_{11A} and H_{11B}

		PRO
		PRO
		PRO

To test hypotheses H_{11A} and $H_{11B,}$ the Arithmetic Means for partitions No. 3, No. 6, and No. 9 (computed under step No. 13) were examined at the 5% and 10% level of significance by using the F-test.

Step No. 31: Test for H_{12A} and H_{12B}

GRO	GRO	GRO

To test hypotheses H_{12A} and H_{12B}, the Arithmetic Means for partitions No. 1, No. 2, and No. 3 (computed under step No. 14) were examined for statistically significant differences at the 5% and 10% level of significance by using the F-test.

Step No. 32: Test for H_{13A} and H_{13B}

PRO	PRO	PRO

To test hypotheses H_{13A} and H_{13B}, the Arithmetic Means for partitions No. 1, No. 2, and No. 3 (computed under step No. 15) were examined for statistically significant differences at the 5% and 10% level of significance by using the F-test.

Step No. 33: Test for H_{14A} and H_{14B}

GRO	GRO	GRO

To test hypotheses H_{14A} and H_{14B}, the Arithmetic Means for partitions No. 4, No. 5, and No. 6 (computed under step No. 16) were examined for statistically significant differences at the 5% and 10% level of significance by using the F-test.

Step No. 34: Test for H_{15A} and H_{15B}

PRO	PRO	PRO

To test hypotheses H_{15A} and H_{15B}, the Arithmetic Means for partitions No. 4, No. 5, and No. 6 (computed under step No. 17) were examined for statistically significant differences at the 5% and 10% level of significance by using the F-test.

Step No. 35: Test for H_{16A} and H_{16B}

GRO	GRO	GRO

To test hypotheses H_{16A} and H_{16B}, the Arithmetic Means for partitions No. 7, No. 8, and No. 9 (computed under step No. 18) were examined for statistically significant differences at the 5% and 10% level of significance by using the F-test.

Step No. 36: Test for H_{17A} and H_{17B}

PRO	PRO	PRO

To test hypotheses H_{17A} and H_{17B}, the Arithmetic Means for partitions No. 7, No. 8, and No. 9 (computed under step No. 19) were examined for statistically significant differences at the 5% and 10% level of significance by using the F-test.

Step No. 37: T-tests

To further explore the relationships between extent of long range planning, bank size, growth trends, and profit trends, large banks are compared to small banks and banks engaging in long range planning to a high extent are compared to banks engaging in long range planning to a low extent. The t-test is used to determine whether or not differences between sample means are significant.

Limitations

This study focuses on the assumption that bank size and extent of long range planning are two important variables affecting profit and growth in the banking industry. Other variables that might affect profit and growth are considered to have a negligible impact or have been isolated through the study design. As one example, results from foreign operations are eliminated from all data used for measurements.

Commercial banks provide a large number of services to their customers. These services, however, can be divided into four broad categories of markets:

a. Security Markets

b. Deposit Markets

c. Loan Markets

d. Markets for a variety of other miscellaneous services (e.g. lock-box, safe deposit box, etc.)[84]

Loan and deposit markets are traditionally the heart of the bank's business,[85] and they constitute the largest contribution to profit in commercial banks. Banking industry sources indicate that this contribution is between 70 and 90 percent.[86] Sunderland (1974) found that current accounts (both loans and deposits) in Swiss banks also represent the largest contribution to profit.[87] Haskins and Sells (1972) state

> The activities of a bank that have to do with deposits, loans, and investments (i.e., its deposit functions, lending functions, and investment functions) are customarily described as "banking operations." This distinguishes them from such "non-banking operations" as trust activities. Although the exact proportions of the total activities that are represented by these banking operations will vary from one bank to another, they will always be high. In many cases they will represent almost the entire activity of the bank.[88]

Because of the magnitude of the contribution of these functions to profit and the wide variety of different services offered by different commercial banks, data from the loan, deposit and investment business of the responding banks will be used as surrogates to measure profit and growth trends. Average deposit figures of the banks will be used to classify the banks by size.

The use of deposits as a measure of growth in commerical banks has been criticized on the grounds that

> . . . total assets, total deposits . . . are inadequate because they are both an immediate reflection of monetary policy, and their slow rate of growth is to be associated with the slow increase of the money supply.[89]

These objections, however, cannot justifiably be raised against this research project. First, all banks included in the study are subject to the same monetary policy constraints. Second, a purpose of the study is to ascertain whether growth is correlated to planning. This research is not concerned with overall growth rates and their causes.

In many industries, annual sales figures are used as a surrogate for growth rates of the company. The sales budget often becomes the basic budget to which all other operations are geared. Plans for purchasing, manufacturing, personnel, research and development, and financing are all synchronized with the forecast of sales volume. What sales are for many industries, deposits are for the banking industry. Harris (1953) states

> . . . in commercial banks, there can be no question as to what constitutes sales. Deposits are sales, and intelligent policies relative to investment cannot be determined until a basic sales budget for deposits has been established.[90]

As deposit and loan functions make the largest contribution to profit in commercial banks, most activities in banks are geared toward deposits and investments in loans and securities.[91] The type and volume of investments are dependent upon the composition and volume of deposits. Composition of deposits (corresponding to product-mix in other industries) mirrors legal and regulatory requirements, volatility, value date, costs, loan-cover, turnover, risk, etc. These and other factors are taken into consideration by bank management when attempting to balance deposits and investments.[92] Harris (1953) and Olson (1964)[93, 94] maintain that deposits are the keystone to planning in commercial banks and all plans for other functions in the bank depend on the deposit function.

For the above stated reasons and because of the uniformity of data guaranteed by the design of the Functional Cost Analysis program, growth trends for banks included in this study are measured by computing changes in average deposits. The source of the average deposit data was the questionnaire used in this study. (Refer to Appendix A.) The data reported by all respondents was prepared according to Functional Cost Analysis guidelines.

Using Functional Cost Analysis data as surrogates for growth and profit trends[95] will limit the generalizability of the findings to medium sized and small banks, since these banks constitute the majority of the participants in the program. The quality of the measurements, however, guaranteed through the use of the Functional Cost Analysis data, will greatly enhance the predictive value of this study. Clearly, no other measurements of growth and profits, used by a large number of banks, provide the same degree of reliability.

The so-called "super-banks" (extremely large banks) are not included in the measurement part of the study, because these banks do not participate in the Functional Cost Analysis program. Comparable growth and profit data are, therefore, not available. This exclusion, however, adds strength to the study. Extremely large banks are very different from small and medium-sized banks in many areas contributing significantly to profits. Homogeneity, and thus comparability, of the surveyed banks in terms of profits will be improved. Stringer Mayne (1967) excluded five Chicago banks with assets of over $500 million for the same reasons.[96] The survey part of the study (the present state of long range planning in commercial banks), however, includes a sample of these large banks in order to obtain information regarding their long range planning practices.

Regulatory agencies,[97, 98] researchers,[99, 100] and the banking industry often use average deposits as the determining criterion for size classifications.[101] The boundaries of the classes, however, vary according to the purpose of the analysis and the amount of detail desired. For this study, the boundaries selected are the same as those used by the Federal Reserve Bank in its Functional Cost Analysis program.[102] Using the same classes as the Functional Cost Analysis program will eliminate distortions otherwise possible and will permit meaningful comparisons with Functional Cost Analysis data.

A time horizon of several years was chosen for this project in order to eliminate, or at least minimize, the impact isolated fluctuations in deposits have on growth trends. The time period of 1970-1974 was selected to eliminate any effects changes in regulatory requirements[103] might have on the data.

The Federal Reserve Act provided for the creation of twelve Federal Reserve districts, each with a Federal Reserve Bank, in order to avoid overconcentration of money power in any one institution. Although the Federal Reserve Banks are located in the important money centers of the United States, the twelve districts differ widely in banking resources and volume of transactions handled.[104] Refer to Table IV-1 for data on total assets and total deposits of each Federal Reserve Bank on December 31, 1974.

To eliminate these inter-district differences and the impact on the data collected, only member banks of the 7th Federal Reserve district,[105] participating in the Functional Cost Analysis program, are considered in this study. Inferences, therefore, will be limited to banks of the 7th Federal Reserve district.

Unequal cell sizes, resulting from the procedures adopted (method of partitioning the banks), will not have any significant effect on the analysis of the data. For a more detailed discussion of the effect of unequal cell sizes refer to Dixon and Massey[106] or any standard text-book in statistics.

Designers of the Functional Cost Analysis program attempted to overcome the problems posed by the unequal number of banks in the different size categories by crossing Federal Reserve district boundaries.

Table IV-1

Total Assets and Total Deposits of Each Federal Reserve Bank on December 31, 1974 (in millions of dollars)

Reserve District	No.	Assets	Deposits
Boston	1	$ 4,748	$ 825
New York	2	28,122	8,235
Philadelphia	3	5,986	1,060
Cleveland	4	8,636	1,713
Richmond	5	6,930	1,893
Atlanta	6	6,930	1,893
Chicago	7	17,448	4,612
St. Louis	8	4,389	1,012
Minneapolis	9	2,729	829
Kansas City	10	4,819	1,340
Dallas	11	5,247	1,896
San Francisco	12	15,481	5,819

Source: Rand McNally, *International Bankers Directory,* Final 1975 Edition, p. P 4.

> For those banks with total deposits up to $50 million, the cost analysis comparisons normally are based on information received only from banks of similar deposit size located within the same Federal Reserve district. For banks with total deposits of $50 million to $200 million, district boundaries may be crossed in order to obtain sufficient banks of this deposit size to develop the comparative averages. For those banks with total deposits over $200 million, Federal Reserve district boundaries are not considered. All banks with total deposits over $200 million are grouped, and the sufficient number of banks required to generate the comparative averages for participating banks of this deposit size is selected from this group.[107]

Any gains in design rigor, achieved through the adoption of crossing class boundaries, or similar procedures, would be more than negated by the data distortions that would be introduced. Crossing class boundaries would ignore environmental and structural differences (such as size, state of economic development, degree of industralization, urban versus rural environment, etc.) between Federal Reserve districts.

In developing the high, moderate, and low long range planning classifications, each *yes* answer to the questionnaire is weighted equally. Although more elaborate weighting scales could perhaps been designed, they would not have added to the rigor of the study design.

Analysis of Long Range Planning Questions

The following section deals with the second part of the study. All data received through the questionnaires were transcribed onto punched cards. *Yes* answers were coded as '1' and *no* answers, or *not applicable*, were coded as 'blanks.' The data then were arranged in such a manner as to allow the use of SPSS (Statistical Package of the Social Sciences) in preparing:

1. A frequency table for each question. Each table includes variable name and label, code (*yes* = 1, *no* or *not applicable* = 0), absolute frequency, relative frequency (in percent), adjusted frequency, cumulative frequency, totals for each column, and several statistical measures, such as a mean, mode, standard deviation, etc.

2. Crosstabulation tables. Each table includes the following information: The names of the two variables (= answers to questions) being "blotted" against each other, a listing and description of all the possible choices for each question that received a *yes* answer, frequency counts for each partition, relative row, column, and entire table frequencies for each partition (in percent), row and column frequency counts, row and column relative frequencies, and several statistical measures such as Chi Square, Cramer's V, contingency Coefficient, etc.

Figure IV-3 presents the "crosstabulation" of the trading area of the bank with the importance of growth as a corporate goal. The trading area is subdivided according to the size of the population that is within a bank's reach:

1. Under 25 thousand
2. 25 thousand but less than 100 thousand

3. 100 thousand but less than 500 thousand

4. 500 thousand and more.

Since none of the respondents indicated a trading area of category 4, it is omitted from the table.

Respondents had the choice of ranking growth as a corporate goal as

1. High

2. Moderate

3. Low

The "Row Total" column indicates the frequency count of responses relative to the trading area. Three banks (3.9% of the total of 77 banks that responded to the questionnaire) did not respond relative to their trading area. Twelve banks (15.6% of 77 responding) reported trading areas of under 25 thousand. Twenty-five banks (32.5% of 77) reported their trading area to be between 25 thousand and 100 thousand, and 37 banks (48.1%) reported a trading area of 100 thousand to 500 thousand. The column totals indicate that all (77) banks answered this question. Twenty-six banks (33.8% of 77) considered the growth goal to be of high importance, 43 banks (55.8% of 77) considered it to be of moderate importance, and 8 banks (10.4% of 77) considered it to be of low importance.

For each partition in the table, the frequency count, the relative row frequency (in percent), column frequency (in percent), and entire table frequency (in percent) is presented. For example: 16 banks reported a trading area of 25 thousand to 100 thousand and moderate importance of growth as a corporate goal. Sixteen banks represent 64% of a total of 25 banks that reported a trading area of 25 thousand to 100 thousand. Sixteen banks also represent 37.2% of a total of 43 banks that reported growth as a goal with moderate importance. And finally, 16 represents 20.8% of 77 banks, the total number of responding banks.

Summary

The purpose of this chapter was to discuss in detail the methodology of the research project. The data collection device—a questionnaire—was traced through the phases of development and testing. Data transformations, modifications, all calculations performed and the statistical testing procedures were presented. Discussions of

Figure IV-3

Crosstabulation

```
STATISTICAL PACKAGE FOR THE SOCIAL SCIENCES SPSSH - RELEASE 6.02            12/28/76     PAGE 10

File    LRP      (creation date = 12/28/76)    Dissertation

                                  C R O S S T A B U L A T I O N   O F
    TRADAREA  TRADING AREA HAS A POPULATION OF:          BY GROWTH    IMPORTANCE OF GROWTH IS:
                                                                                      Page 1 of 1
                   Growth
              CountI
            Row PctI  High       Moderate  low        Row
            Col PctI                                  Total
            Tot PctI        1.I          2.I       3.I
Tradarea    -------I---------I----------I--------I
                 0. I       2 I         1 I       0 I    3
                    I    66.7 I      33.3 I     0.0 I  3.9
                    I     7.7 I       2.3 I     0.0 I
                    I     2.6 I       1.3 I     0.0 I
                   -I---------I----------I--------I
                 1. I       6 I         5 I       1 I   12
Under     25th      I    50.0 I      41.7 I     8.3 I 15.6
                    I    23.1 I      11.6 I    12.5 I
                    I     7.8 I       6.5 I     1.3 I
                   -I---------I----------I--------I
                 2. I       8 I        16 I       1 I   25
25th - 100th        I    32.0 I      64.0 I     4.0 I 32.5
                    I    30.8 I      37.2 I    12.5 I
                    I    10.4 I      20.8 I     1.3 I
                   -I---------I----------I--------I
                 3. I      10 I        21 I       6 I   37
100th - 500th       I    27.0 I      56.8 I    16.2 I 48.1
                    I    38.5 I      48.8 I    75.0 I
                    I    13.0 I      27.3 I     7.8 I
                   -I---------I----------I--------I
            column        26          43         8     77
             total      33.8        55.8      10.4  100.0

CHI SQUARE =  5.97842 with 6 degrees of freedom significance =  0.4256
CRAMER'S V =  0.19703
CONTINGENCY COEFFICIENT =  0.26842
LAMBDA (ASYMMETRIC)  =  0.0     with Tradarea Dependent.     =   0.05882 with growth  dependent.
LAMBDA (SYMMETRIC)  =  0.02703
UNCERTAINTY COEFFICIENT (ASYMMETRIC)  =  0.03548 with Tradarea Dependent.  =  0.04338 with growth dependent.
UNCERTAINTY COEFFICIENT (SYMMETRIC) =  0.03904
KENDALL'S TAU B  =  0.20202  SIGNIFICANCE  =  0.0264
KENDALL'S TAU B  CANNOT BE COMPUTED
KENDALL'S TAU C  =  0.18165  SIGNIFICANCE  =  0.0264
GAMMA =     0.33272
SOMERS'S D (ASYMMETRIC)  =  0.21497 with Tradarea Dependent.    =  0.18985 with growth dependent.
SOMERS'S D (SYMMETRIC)  =  0.20163
```

general limitations and the analysis of the long range planning data concluded Chapter IV. The following chapter will present the results of the hypotheses testing.

CHAPTER V

TEST OF HYPOTHESES AND DATA ANALYSIS

Introduction

This chapter presents analyses of empirical data gathered for the study and the results of all relevant hypotheses. The empirical data consist of profit and growth data for the period of 1970-1974 and information on long range planning on the participants in this project. (A description of the methodology employed has been presented in Chapter IV.)

One purpose of this study has been to investigate the relationship between long range planning efforts and growth and profit trends in commercial banks. Growth and profit trends are derived from Functional Cost Analysis program data. The extent of long range planning effort was determined through the use of a questionnaire. The test of the significance of the relationship between these trends and the extent of long range planning was based on the premise that long range planning is one of the important variables affecting growth and profit in commercial banks.

The data collected were used to test several hypotheses which were formulated for the study. These hypotheses were designed to examine the following areas of relationships:

1. Bank size and extent of long range planning efforts undertaken
2. Bank size and trends for growth and profit
3. Extent of long range planning and trends for growth and profit
4. Extent of long range planning, bank size and trends for growth and profit.

Results of Hypotheses Testing

The design of this study requires that important characteristics of several sub-groups of banks be examined simultaneously. For reasons discussed in Chapter IV, the analysis of variance was selected as the appropriate procedure to perform statistical tests of the hypotheses formulated for this research. A detailed discussion of the analysis of variance procedure is included in Appendix F.

Relationship of Bank Size and Extent of LRP

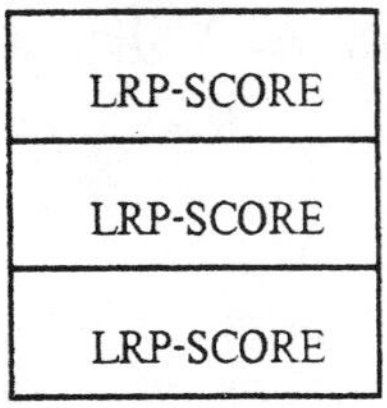

One of the goals of the study is to determine whether the extent of long range planning undertaken by commercial banks changes when bank size increases or decreases. In order to examine this relationship, the following hypotheses are statistically tested. H_{1A}: Banks of size 'A' do not engage in significantly more long range planning (LRP) than do banks of size 'B.' H_{1B}: Banks of size 'B' do not engage in significantly more LRP than do banks of size 'C.'

The analysis of variance permits the test of whether the means of sub-samples, into which the sample data are broken, are significantly different from each other. To test hypotheses H_{1A} and H_{1B}, the mean LRP-Scores ($\overline{X}_1$, $\overline{X}_2$, and $\overline{X}_3$) for the banks in the three size classes (A = large, B = medium, C = small) are computed.

Table V-1 presents an analysis of variance table for LRP-Scores for banks of sizes A, B, and C. The table summarizes the results of the analysis of variance of hypotheses H_{1A} and H_{1B}. Columns (1), (2), and (3), respectively, list the possible sources of variation, the sum of squares for each of these sources, and the number of degrees of freedom associated with each of the sums of squares. Column (2) divided by Column (3) yields the between groups mean squares (MS_b) and within groups mean squares (MS_w) shown in Column (4). The F-Ratio is the result of dividing MS_b by MS_w. The table also presents the critical F-value at the 5% level of significance.

Standard reference tables of critical values for F-Ratios indicate for F with 2 degrees of freedom for MS_b (numerator) and 74 degrees of freedom for MS_b (denominator) at the 5% level of statistical significance a critial value of 3.1300.[108] Since the computed F-value for hypotheses H_{1A} and H_{1B} (refer to Table V-1) is equal to 2.0720, and thus smaller than the critical value of 3.1300, the null hypothesis cannot be rejected.

The conclusion of testing Hypothesis No. 1 then is that the group sample means (LRP-Scores for banks of sizes A, B, and C) are not significantly different from each other. The immediate inference to be made from this test is that the extent of long range planning a bank undertakes does not seem to be dependent on bank size.

Relationship of Bank Size and Trends for Growth and Profit

The immediately preceding section explored the relationship of bank size and extent of long range planning activities. To further assess the impact bank size might have on the bank characteristics under examination in this study, hypotheses $H_{2A,B}$ and $H_{3A,B}$ are being tested below.

Hypotheses $H_{2A,B}$ and $H_{3A,B}$ examine the relationship between bank size and trends for growth and profit. The hypotheses focus on bank size as the important variable affecting growth and profit trends.

H_{2A}: Banks of size 'A' do not experience significantly higher percentage changes in growth than do banks of size 'B.'

H_{2B}: Banks of size 'B' do not experience significantly higher percentage changes in growth than do banks of size 'C.'

H_{3A}: Banks of size 'A' do not experience significantly higher percentage changes in profit than do banks of size 'B.'

H_{3B}: Banks of size 'B' do not experience significantly higher percentage changes in profit than do banks of size 'C.'

Test results for the above hypotheses are presented in Table V-2 and Table V-3.

Reference to Critical Value Tables indicates for (F2,56) at the 5% level of statistical significance a critical value of 3.1660. The computed F-value for hypotheses $H_{2A,B}$ is 4.9239 (refer to Table V-2). Since the computed F-value is greater than the critical F-value, the null hypothesis is rejected.

The conclusion of the test of Hypothesis No. 2 is that the group sample means (changes of growth for banks of sizes A, B, and C) are significantly different from each other. Banks size seems to influence growth rates in commercial banks.

The computed F-value for Hypotheses $H_{3A,B}$ is 0.2171 (refer to Table V-3). The critical F-value for F(2,56) at the 5% level of statistical significance is 3.1660. The computed F-value is smaller than the critical F-value. The null hypothesis cannot be rejected.

The test of Hypothesis No. 3 indicates that the group sample means (changes in profit for banks of sizes A, B, and C) are not significantly different from each other. Bank profits do not seem to be influenced significantly by bank size.

Extent of LRP and Trends for Growth and Profit

The principal theme of inquiry of this study is the impact of long range planning on success in commercial banks. Success is represented by growth and profit. A survey of the literature (refer to Chapter II) has revealed that growth and profit play a very important role in the banking industry and the nation's economy. Several studies suggested that planning technques, successfully used in other industries, could be applied in commercial banks. These techniques could help solve the problem that declining profits present for the banking industry and ultimately for the economy as a whole.

To determine whether success, represented by growth and profit trends in this study, is correlated to the extent of long range planning efforts undertaken by banks, Hypotheses $H_{4A,B}$ and $H_{5A,B}$ are tested below. These hypotheses focus on the extent of long range planning as the important variable affecting growth and profit trends.

H_{4A}: Banks engaging to a high degree in LRP do not experience significantly higher changes in growth than do banks engaging to a moderate degree in LRP.

H_{4B}: Banks engaging to a moderate degree in LRP do not experience significantly higher changes in growth than do banks engaging to a low degree in LRP.

H_{5A}: Banks engaging to a high degree in LRP do not experience significantly higher changes in profit than do banks engaging to a moderate degree in LRP.

H_{5B}: Banks engaging to a moderate degree in LRP do not experience significantly higher changes in profit than do banks engaging to a low degree in LRP.

Test results for the above hypotheses are presented in Tables V-4 and V-5.

Reference to Critical Value Tables for F-Ratios indicates for F(2,56) a critical value of 3.1660. The computed F-value for Hypotheses $H_{4A,B}$ is 0.7699 (refer to Table V-4). Since the computed F-value is smaller than the critical F-value, the null hypothesis cannot be rejected.

The test of Hypothesis No. 4 indicates that the group sample means (changes in growth for banks of high, moderate, and low long range planning extent) are not significantly different from each other. Extent of LRP does not seem to influence changes in growth significantly.

The computed F-value for Hypotheses $H_{5A,B}$ is 0.3355 (refer to Table V-5). The critical value for F(2,56) at the 5% level of statistical significance is 3.1660. Since the computed F-value is smaller than the critical F-value, the null hypothesis cannot be rejected.

The test of Hypothesis No. 5 indicates that the group sample means (changes in profit for banks of high, moderate, and low LRP extent) are not significantly different from each other. Extent of LRP does not seem to influence changes in profit significantly.

Extent of LRP, Bank Size, Trends for Growth and Profit

The immediately preceding section examined the relationship of extend of LRP and trends for growth and profit. As stated earlier, this relationship is the fulcrum of the research project. To further examine the relationship between extent of LRP and success, bank size is introduced in this section.

All hypotheses in this section examine the relationship between the extent of long range planning, bank size and trends for growth and profit. $H_{6A,B}$ through $H_{11A,B}$ examine the relationship of different sized banks having the same extent of long range planning and trends for growth and profit. Hypotheses $H_{12A,B}$ through $H_{17A,B}$ examine the relationship of banks of the same size which have exhibited differing extents of long range planning and trends for growth and profit.

This set of hypotheses focusses on the extent of long range planning and bank size as the important variable affecting growth and profit trends.

H_{6A}: Banks in cell No. 1 do not experience significantly different percentage changes in growth than do banks in cell No. 4.

H_{6B}: Banks in cell No. 4 do not experience significantly different percentage changes in growth than do banks in cell No. 7.

H_{7A}: Banks in cell No. 1 do not experience significantly different percentage changes in profit than do banks in cell No. 4.

H_{7B}: Banks in cell No. 4 do not experience significantly different percentage changes in profit than do banks in cell No. 7.

H_{8A}: Banks in cell No. 2 do not experience significantly different percentage changes in growth than do banks in cell No. 5.

H_{8B}: Banks in cell No. 5 do not experience significantly different percentage changes in growth than do banks in cell No. 8.

H_{9A}: Banks in cell No. 2 do not experience significantly different percentage changes in profit than do banks in cell No. 5.

H_{9B}: Banks in cell No. 5 do not experience significantly different percentage changes in profit than do banks in cell No. 8.

H_{10A}: Banks in cell No. 3 do not experience significantly different percentage changes in growth than do banks in cell No. 6.

H_{10B}: Banks in cell No. 6 do not experience significantly different percentage changes in growth than do banks in cell No. 9.

H_{11A}: Banks in cell No. 3 do not experience significantly different percentage changes in profit than do banks in cell No. 6.

H_{11B}: Banks in cell No. 6 do not experience significantly different percentage changes in profit than do banks in cell No. 9.

H_{12A}: Banks of size 'A' engaging to a high degree in LRP (banks in cell No. 1) do not experience significantly different percentage changes in growth than do banks of size 'A' engaging to a moderate degree in LRP (banks in cell No. 2).

H_{12B}: Banks in cell No. 2 do not experience significantly different percentage changes in growth than do banks in cell No. 3.

H_{13A}: Banks in cell No. 1 do not experience significantly different percentage changes in profit than do banks in cell No. 2.

H_{13B}: Banks in cell No. 2 do not experience significantly different percentage changes in profit than do banks in cell No. 3.

H_{14A}: Banks in cell No. 4 do not experience significantly different percentage changes in growth than do banks in cell No. 5.

H_{14B}: Banks in cell No. 5 do not experience significantly different percentage changes in growth than do banks in cell No. 6.

H_{15A}: Banks in cell No. 4 do not experience significantly different percentage changes in profit than do banks in cell No. 5.

H_{15B}: Banks in cell No. 5 do not experience significantly different percentage changes in profit than do banks in cell No. 6.

H_{16A}: Banks in cell no. 7 do not experience significantly different percentage changes in growth than do banks in cell No. 8.

H_{16B}: Banks in cell No. 8 do not experience significantly different percentage changes in growth than do banks in cell No. 9.

H_{17A}: Banks in cell No. 7 do not experience significantly different percentage changes in profit than do banks in cell No. 8.

H_{17B}: Banks in cell No. 8 do not experience significantly different percentage changes in profit than do banks in cell No. 9.

Test results for the above hypotheses are presented in Table V-6 through Table V-17.

Reference to Critical Value Tables for F-Ratios indicates for F(2,17) a critial value of 3.6040. The computed F-value for Hypotheses $H_{6A,B}$ is 7.9688 (refer to Table V-6). Since the computed F-value is greater than the critical F-value, the null hypothesis is rejected.

The test of Hypothesis No. 6 indicates that the group sample means (changes in growth for banks of high LRP extent and sizes A, B, and C) are significantly different from each other. Bank size thus seems to influence changes in growth in banks engaging to a high extent in LRP activities.

The computed F-value for Hypotheses $H_{7A,B}$ is 1.0639 (refer to Table V-7). The critical value for F(2,17) at the 5% level of statistical significance is 3.6040. Since the computed F-value is smaller than the critical F-value, the null hypothesis cannot be rejected.

The test of Hypothesis No. 7 indicates that the group sample means (changes in profit for banks of high LRP extent and sizes A, B, and C) are not significantly different from each other. Bank size does not seem to influence changes in profit in banks engaging to a high extent in LRP activities.

Critical Value Tables for F-Ratios indicate for F(2,21) a critical value of 3.4375. The computed F-value for Hypotheses $H_{8A,B}$ is 0.7291 (refer to Table V-8). Since the computed F-value is smaller than the critical F-value, the null hypothesis cannot be rejected.

The test of Hypothesis No. 8 indicates that the group sample means (changes in growth for banks of moderate LRP extent and sizes A, B, and C) are not significantly different from each other. Bank size does not seem to influence changes in growth in banks engaging to a moderate extent in LRP activities.

The computed F-value for Hypotheses $H_{9A,B}$ is 0.2271 (refer to Table V-9). The critical value for F(2,21) at the 5% level of statistical significance is 3.4675. Since the computed F-value is smaller than the critical F-value, the null hypothesis cannot be rejected.

The test of Hypothesis No. 9 indicates that the group sample means (changes in profit for banks of moderate LRP extent and sizes A, B, and C) are not significantly different from each other. Bank size does not seem to influence changes in profit in banks engaging to a moderate extent in LRP activities.

Critical Value Tables for F-Ratios indicate for F(1,13) a critical value of 4.6800. The computed F-value for Hypotheses $H_{10A,B}$ is 0.2045 (refer to Table V-10). Since the computed F-value is smaller than the critical F-value, the null hypothesis cannot be rejected.

The test of Hypothesis No. 10 indicates that the group sample means (changes in growth for banks of low LRP extent and sizes A, B, and C) are not significantly different from each other. Bank size does not seem to influence changes in growth in banks engaging to a low extent in LRP activities.

The computed F-value for Hypotheses $H_{11A,B}$ is 0.3517 (refer to Table V-11). The critical value for F(1,13) at the 5% level of statistical significance is 4.4800. Since the computed F-value is smaller than the critical F-value, the null hypothesis cannot be rejected.

The test of Hypothesis No. 11 indicates that the group sample means (changes in profit for banks of low LRP extent and sizes A, B, and C) are not significantly different from each other. Bank sizes does not seem to influence changes in profit in banks engaging to a low extent in LRP activities.

Critical Value Tables for F-Ratios indicate for F(1,7) a critical value of 5.5900. The computed F-value for Hypotheses $H_{12A,B}$ is 2.1721 (refer to Table V-12). Since the computed F-value is smaller than the critical F-value, the null hypothesis cannot be rejected.

The test of Hypothesis No. 12 indicates that the group sample means (changes in growth for banks of size A engaging in LRP to high, moderate and low extent) are not significantly different from each other. LRP extent does not seem to influence changes in growth in banks of size A to a significant degree.

The computed F-value for Hypotheses $H_{13A,B}$ is 1.2638 (refer to Table V-13). The critical value for F(1,7) at the 5% level of statistical significance is 5.5900. Since the computed F-value is smaller than the critical F-value, the null hypothesis cannot be rejected.

The test of Hypothesis No. 13 indicates that the group sample means (changes in profit for banks of size A engaging in LRP to high, moderate, and low extent) are not significantly different from each other. LRP seems not to influence changes in profit in banks of size A to a significant degree.

Critical Value Tables for F-Ratios indicate for F(2,26) a critical value of 3.3734. The computed F-value for Hypotheses $H_{14A,B}$ is 0.5463 (refer to Table V-14). Since the computed F-value is smaller than the critical F-value, the null hypothesis cannot be rejected.

The test of Hypothesis No. 14 indicates that the group sample means (changes in growth for banks of size B engaging to high, moderate, and low extent in LRP) are not significantly different from each other. LRP extent does not seem to influence changes in growth in banks of size B to a significant degree.

The computed F-value for Hypotheses $H_{15A,B}$ is 0.4704 (refer to Table V-15). The critical value for F(2,26) at the 5% level of statistical significance is 3.3734. Since the computed F-value is smaller than the critical F-value, the null hypothesis cannot be rejected.

The test of Hypothesis No. 15 indicates that the group sample means (changes in profit for banks of size B engaging in LRP to high, moderate and low extent) are not significantly different from each other. LRP extent does not seem to influence changes in profit in banks of size B to a significant degree.

Critical Value Tables for F-Ratios indicate for F(2,18) a critical value of 3.5660. The computed F-value for Hypotheses $H_{16A,B}$ is 2.3757 (refer to Table V-16). Since the computed F-value is smaller than the critical F-value, the null hypothesis cannot be rejected.

The test of Hypothesis No. 16 indicates that the group sample means (changes in growth for banks of size C engaging in LRP to high, moderate and low extent) are not significantly different from each other. LRP extent does not seem to influence changes in growth in banks of size C to a significant degree.

The computed F-value for Hypotheses $H_{17A,B}$ is 0.6174 (refer to Table V-17). The critical value for F(2,18) at the 5% level of statistical significance is 3.5660. Since the computed F-value is smaller than the critical F-value, the null hypothesis cannot be rejected.

The test of Hypothesis No. 17 indicates that the group sample means (changes in profit for banks of Size C engaging in LRP to high, moderate, and low extent) are not significantly different from each other. LRP extent does not seem to influence changes in profit in banks of size C to a significant degree.

Summary of Test Results

The results of the hypotheses tests are summarized in Table V-18. The first column in the table identifies the hypothesis, the second column presents the computed F-values for each hypothesis and the third column presents the critical F-values at the 5% level of statistical significance. The fourth column indicates whether the null hypothesis has been accepted or rejected.

The results of testing the four groups of relationships:

1. Bank size and extent of long range planning efforts undertaken;
2. Banks size and trends for growth and profit;
3. Extent of long range planning and trends for growth and profit;
4. Extent of long range planning, bank size and trends for growth and profit;

indicate that bank size seems to have a significant impact on changes in growth in banks (refer to Table V-2). The results further show that this significant impact occurs only among banks that engage to a high extent in LRP (refer to Table V-6). The data analysis did not reveal any significant relationships between banks size, extent of LRP and changes in profit.

Discussion of T-Tests

As discussed earlier, the study was designed to examine subgroups of commercial banks. The preceding sections presented the test results of hypotheses comprising all banks included in the study. The purpose of the following section is to describe comparisons that are limited to the following groups of banks:

1. large and small banks
2. banks engaging in long range planning to a high or to a low extent.

Consequently medium (size) banks and banks engaging to a moderate extent in long range planning are excluded from the analysis that follows.

The above mentioned comparisons are included to provide further information about the relationships between the extent to which banks engage in long range planning, size, growth trends, and profit trends. If differences in growth and profit trends exist between the subgroups of banks included in this study, it is reasonable to expect that the greatest differences might occur between large and small banks and banks engaging in long range planning to a high extent and to a low extent.

Since all of the following tests involve the comparison of growth or profit trends of two subsamples of commercial banks, the analysis of variance procedure cannot be used. Instead, the appropriate statistical procedure for testing whether or not the difference between two sample means is significant is the t-test. (For further details on the t-test refer to any standard textbook.)

The results of these t-tests are summarized in Table V-19. The first and third column of the table identify the subsamples that are being compared. Columns three and four present the computed and critical t-values for each comparison. For example, Columns one and two of the second line in Table V-19 present the results of comparing growth trends of large banks to growth trends of small banks.

The computed t-value of 1.968 is smaller than the critical t-value of 2.048 at the 5% level of signficance. The computed t-value of 1.968, however, is larger than the critical t-value of 1.701 at the 10% level of signficance. Therefore, the null hypothesis (the means of the two groups are equal) is accepted at the 5% level and rejected at the 10% level. Columns three and four of the second line present the results of comparing profit trends of large banks to profit trends of small banks. Since the computed t-value of 0.152 is smaller than the critical t-value of 2.048, the null hypothesis cannot be rejected at the 5% level of significance. The remaining results follow the same pattern.

The t-tests indicate that growth trends experienced by large banks engaging to a high extent in long range planning are significantly different from growth trends experienced by small banks engaging to a high extent in long range planning. This result confirms the test results of Hypotheses $H_{6A,B}$.

The tests also indicate that growth trends experienced by small banks engaging to a high extent in long range planning are significantly different from growth trends experienced by small banks engaging to a low extent in long range planning. (Compare to results of testing Hypotheses $H_{16A,B}$.) The t-tests did not reveal significant differences between profit trends experienced by the various subgroups of banks.

Summary

This chapter presented the results of hypotheses testing. The tests comprised seventeen hypotheses which examine the relationships between banks size and extent of long range planning efforts undertaken, bank size and trends for growth and profit, extent of long range planning and trends for growth and profit, extent of long range planning, bank size, and trends for growth and profit. Analysis of Variance Tables presented statistical information for each of the seventeen hypotheses. The chapter concluded with a summary of t-test results. These tests compared large banks to small banks and banks engaging in long range planning to a high extent to banks engaging in long range planning to a low extent.

The purpose of Chapter VI is to present a summary of the study and the interpretations and conclusions derived from this empirical research. Suggestions for further research are also discussed.

Table V-1

Analysis of Variance Table of LRP-Scores for Banks of Sizes A, B, and C.

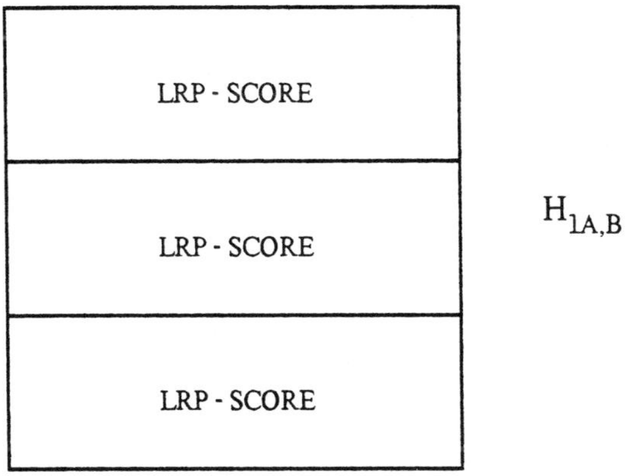

(1) SOURCE OF VARIATION	(2) SUM OF SQUARES	(3) DEGREES OF FREEDOM	(4) MEAN SQUARE
Between Groups	688.4805	(2)	344.3402
Within Groups	12294.3398	(74)	166.1397
Total	12982.8203	(76)	

$$F(2,74) = \frac{344.3402}{166.1397} = 2.072$$

Critical F-value (5% level of significance)

$F(2,74) = 3.13$

Table V-2

Analysis of Variance Table of Trends for Growth for Banks of Sizes A, B, and C.

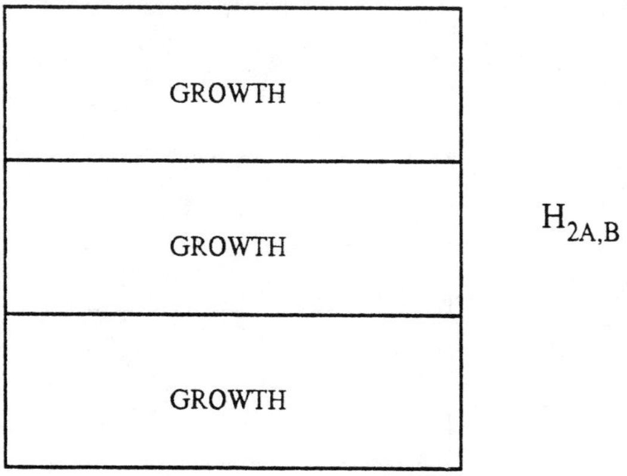

(1) SOURCE OF VARIATION	(2) SUM OF SQUARES	(3) DEGREES OF FREEDOM	(4) MEAN SQUARE
Between Groups	147.9092	(2)	73.9546
Within Groups	841.0869	(56)	15.0194
Total	988.9961	(58)	

$$F(2,56) = \frac{73.9546}{15.0194} = 4.9239$$

Critical F-value (5% level of significance)

$$F(2,56) = 3.1660$$

Table V-3

Analysis of Variance Table of Trends for Profit for Banks of Sizes A, B, and C.

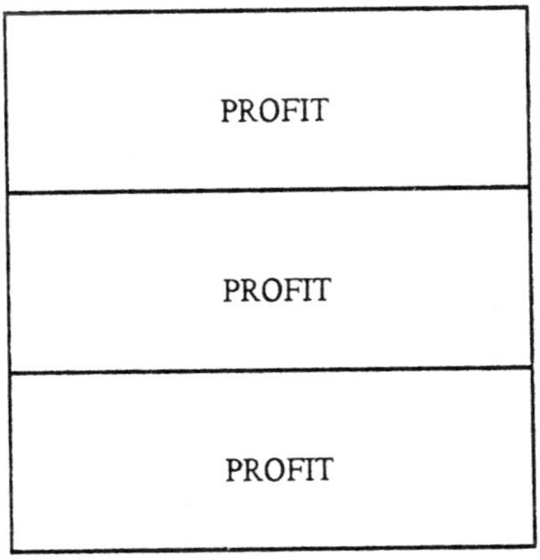

$H_{3A,B}$

(1) SOURCE OF VARIATION	(2) SUM OF SQUARES	(3) DEGREES OF FREEDOM	(4) MEAN SQUARE
Between groups	57.4922	(2)	28.7461
Within Groups	7413.3359	(56)	132.3810
Total	7470.8281	(58)	

$$F(2,56) = \frac{28.7461}{132.3810} = 0.2171$$

Critical Value for F (5% level of significance)

$F(2,56) = 3.1660$

Table V-4

Analysis of Variance Table of Trends for Growth for Banks of High, Moderate, and Low LRP-Extent.

GROWTH	GROWTH	GROWTH	$H_{4A,B}$

(1) SOURCE OF VARIATION	(2) SUM OF SQUARES	(3) DEGREES OF FREEDOM	(4) MEAN SQUARE
Between Groups	26.4675	(2)	13.2338
Within Groups	962.5247	(56)	17.1879
Total	988.9922	(58)	

$$F(2,56) = \frac{13.2338}{17.1879} = 0.7699$$

Critical F-value (5% level of significance)

$F(2,56) = 3.1660$

Table V-5

Analysis of Variance Table of Trends for Profit for Banks of High, Moderate, and Low LRP-Extent

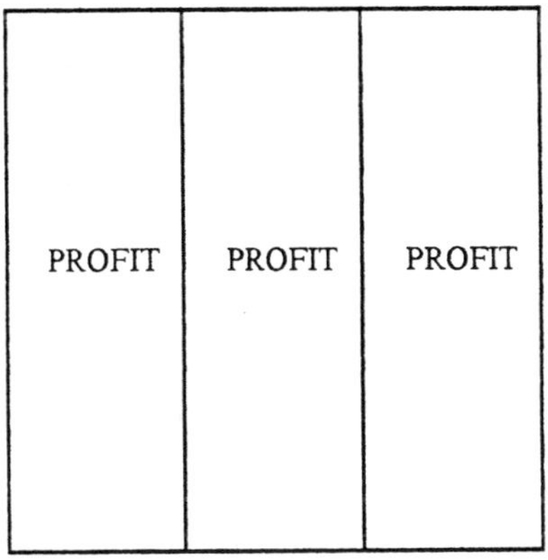

$H_{5A,B}$

(1) SOURCE OF VARIATION	(2) SUM OF SQUARES	(3) DEGREES OF FREEDOM	(4) MEAN SQUARE
Between Groups	88.4609	(2)	44.2305
Within Groups	7382.3672	(56)	131.8280
Total	7470.8281	(58)	

$$F(2,56) = \frac{44.2305}{131.8280} = 0.3355$$

Critical F-value (5% level of significance)

$F(2,56) = 3.1660$

Table V-6

Analysis of Variance Table of Trends for Growth for Banks of High LRP-Extent and Sizes A, B, and C.

GROWTH		
GROWTH		
GROWTH		

$H_{6A,B}$

(1) SOURCE OF VARIATION	(2) SUM OF SQUARES	(3) DEGREES OF FREEDOM	(4) MEAN SQUARE
Between Groups	204.4245	(2)	102.2122
Within Groups	218.0518	(17)	12.8266
Total	422.4763	(19)	

$$F(2,17) = \frac{102.2122}{12.8266} = 7.9688$$

Critical F-value (5% level of significance)

$F(2,17) = 3.6040$

Table V-7

Analysis of Variance Table of Trends for Profit for Banks of High LRP-Extent and Sizes A, B, and C.

PROFIT		
PROFIT		
PROFIT		

$H_{8A,B}$

(1) SOURCE OF VARIATION	(2) SUM OF SQUARES	(3) DEGREES OF FREEDOM	(4) MEAN SQUARE
Between Groups	290.1880	(2)	145.0940
Within Groups	2318.5291	(17)	136.3840
Total	2608.7170	(19)	

$$F(2,17) = \frac{145.0940}{136.3840} = 1.0639$$

Critical F-value (5% level of significance)

$F(2,17) = 3.604$

Table V-8

Analysis of Variance Table of Trends for Growth for Banks of Moderate LRP-Extent and Sizes A, B, and C.

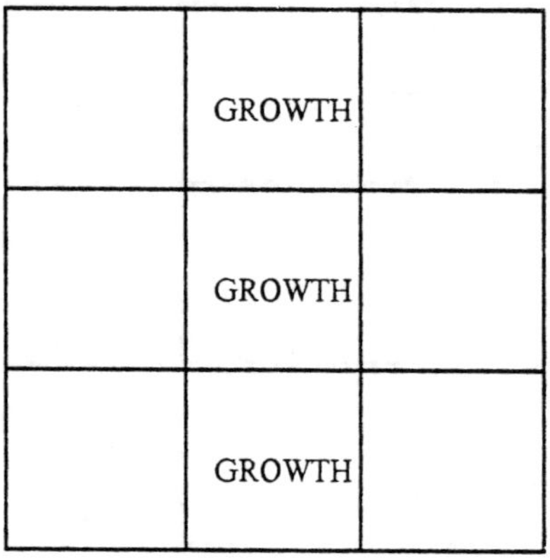

$H_{8A,B}$

(1) SOURCE OF VARIATION	(2) SUM OF SQUARES	(3) DEGREES OF FREEDOM	(4) MEAN SQUARE
Between Groups	20.6521	(2)	10.3260
Within Groups	297.4216	(21)	14.1629
Total	318.0737	(23)	

$$F(2,21) = \frac{10.3260}{14.1629} = 0.7291$$

Critical F-value (5% level of significance)

$F(2,21) = 3.4675$

Table V-9

Analysis of Variance Table of Trends for Profit for Banks of Moderate LRP-Extent and Sizes A, B, and C.

	PROFIT	
	PROFIT	
	PROFIT	

$H_{9A,B}$

(1) SOURCE OF VARIATION	(2) SUM OF SQUARES	(3) DEGREES OF FREEDOM	(4) MEAN SQUARE
Between Groups	37.2847	(2)	18.6423
Within Groups	1723.9421	(21)	82.0925
Total	1761.2268	(23)	

$$F(2,21) = \frac{18.6423}{82.0925} = 0.2271$$

Critical F-value (5% level of significance)

$$F(2,21) = 3.4675$$

Table V-10

Analysis of Variance Table of Trends for Growth for Banks of Low LRP-Extent and Sizes A, B, and C.

		GROWTH
		GROWTH
		GROWTH

$H_{10A,B}$

(1) SOURCE OF VARIATION	(2) SUM OF SQUARES	(3) DEGREES OF FREEDOM	(4) MEAN SQUARE
Between Groups	3.4382	(1)	3.4382
Within Groups	218.5261	(13)	16.8097
Total	221.9644	(14)	

$$F(1,13) = \frac{3.4382}{16.8097} = 0.2045$$

Critical F-value (5% level of significance)

$F(1,13) = 4.6800$

Table V-11

Analysis of Variance Table of Trends for Profit for Banks of Low LRP-Extent and Sizes A, B, and C.

		PROFIT
		PROFIT
		PROFIT

$H_{11A,B}$

(1) SOURCE OF VARIATION	(2) SUM OF SQUARES	(3) DEGREES OF FREEDOM	(4) MEAN SQUARE
Between Groups	79.3574	(1)	79.3574
Within Groups	2933.0911	(13)	225.6224
Total	3012.4485	(14)	

$$F(1,13) = \frac{79.3574}{225.6224} = 0.3517$$

Critical F-value (5% level of significance)

$F(1,13) = 4.6800$

Table V-12

Analysis of Variance Table of Trends for Growth for Banks of Size A and High, Moderate, and Low LRP-Extent.

GROWTH	GROWTH	GROWTH

$H_{12A,B}$

(1) SOURCE OF VARIATION	(2) SUM OF SQUARES	(3) DEGREES OF FREEDOM	(4) MEAN SQUARE
Between Groups	25.1752	(1)	25.1752
Within Groups	81.1307	(7)	11.5901
Total	106.3059	(8)	

$$F(1,7) = \frac{25.1752}{11.5901} = 2.1721$$

Critical F-value (5% level of significance)

$F(1,7) = 5.5900$

Table V-13

Analysis of Variance Table of Trends for Profit for Banks of Size A and High, Moderate, and Low LRP-Extent.

PROFIT	PROFIT	PROFIT

$H_{13A,B}$

(1) SOURCE OF VARIATION	(2) SUM OF SQUARES	(3) DEGREES OF FREEDOM	(4) MEAN SQUARE
Between Groups	66.9844	(1)	66.9844
Within Groups	371.0103	(7)	53.0015
Total	473.9946	(8)	

$$F(1,7) = \frac{66.9844}{53.0015} = 1.2638$$

Critical F-value (5% level of significance)

$F(1,7) = 5.5900$

Table V-14

Analysis of Variance Table of Trends for Growth for Banks of Size B and High, Moderate, and Low LRP-Extent.

GROWTH	GROWTH	GROWTH

$H_{14A,B}$

(1) SOURCE OF VARIATION	(2) SUM OF SQUARES	(3) DEGREES OF FREEDOM	(4) MEAN SQUARE
Between Groups	17.1238	(2)	8.5619
Within Groups	407.4705	(26)	15.6719
Total	424.5942	(28)	

$F(2,26) = \frac{8.5619}{15.6719} = 0.5463$

Critical F-value (5% level of significance)

$F(2,26) = 3.3734$

Table V-15

Analysis of Variance Table of Trends for Profit for Banks of Size B and High, Moderate, and Low LRP-Extent

PROFIT	PROFIT	PROFIT

$H_{15A,B}$

(1) SOURCE OF VARIATION	(2) SUM OF SQUARES	(3) DEGREES OF FREEDOM	(4) MEAN SQUARE
Between Groups	91.8328	(2)	45.9164
Within Groups	2538.0010	(26)	97.6154
Total	2629.8337	(28)	

$$F(2,26) = \frac{45.9164}{97.6154} = 0.4704$$

Critical F-value (5% level of significance)

$F(2,26) = 3.3734$

Table V-16

Analysis of Variance Table of Trends for Growth for Banks of Size C and High, Moderate, and Low LRP-Extent

GROWTH	GROWTH	GROWTH

$H_{16A,B}$

(1) SOURCE OF VARIATION	(2) SUM OF SQUARES	(3) DEGREES OF FREEDOM	(4) MEAN SQUARE
Between Groups	64.7781	(2)	32.3890
Within Groups	245.3984	(18)	13.6332
Total	310.1765	(20)	

$$F(2,18) = \frac{32.3890}{13.6332} = 2.3757$$

Critical F-value (5% level of significance)

$F(2,18) = 3.5660$

Table V-17

Analysis of Variance Table of Trends for Profit for Banks of Size C and High, Moderate, and Low LRP-Extent

PROFIT	PROFIT	PROFIT

$H_{17A,B}$

(1) SOURCE OF VARIATION	(2) SUM OF SQUARES	(3) DEGREES OF FREEDOM	(4) MEAN SQUARE
Between Groups	278.9802	(2)	139.4901
Within Groups	4066.5510	(18)	225.9195
Total	4345.5312	(20)	

$$F(2,18) = \frac{139.4901}{225.9195} = 0.6174$$

Critical F-value (5% level of significance)

$F(2,18) = 3.5660$

Table V-18

Summary of Hypotheses Testing
(Critical F-values at 5% Level of Significance)

Hypothesis	Computed F-Value	Critical F-Value	Hypothesis accepted (rejected)
$H_{1A,B}$	2.0720	3.1300	accepted
$H_{2A,B}$	4.9239	3.1660	(rejected)
$H_{3A,B}$	0.2171	3.1660	accepted
$H_{4A,B}$	0.7699	3.1660	accepted
$H_{5A,B}$	0.3355	3.1660	accepted
$H_{6A,B}$	7.9688	3.6040	(rejected)
$H_{7A,B}$	1.0639	3.6040	accepted
$H_{8A,B}$	0.7291	3.4675	accepted
$H_{9A,B}$	0.2271	3.4675	accepted
$H_{10A,B}$	0.2045	4.6800	accepted
$H_{11A,B}$	0.3517	4.6800	accepted
$H_{12A,B}$	2.1721	5.5900	accepted
$H_{13A,B}$	1.2638	5.5900	accepted
$H_{14A,B}$	0.5463	3.3734	accepted
$H_{15A,B}$	0.4704	3.3734	accepted
$H_{16A,B}$	2.3757	3.5660	accepted
$H_{17A,B}$	0.6174	3.5660	accepted

Table V-19

Summary of T-Tests Critical T-values at 5% Level of Significance, Unless Otherwise Indicated.

Subgroups	Computed (Critical) T-values	Subgroups	Computed (Critical) T-values
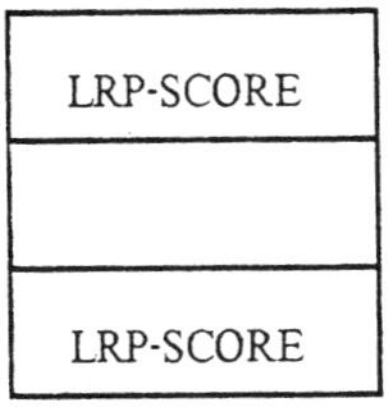	1.308 (2.020)		
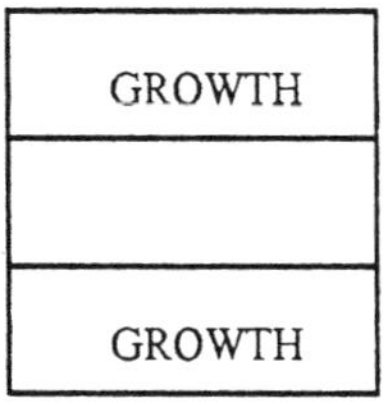	1.968 ** (2.048) (1.701) 10%	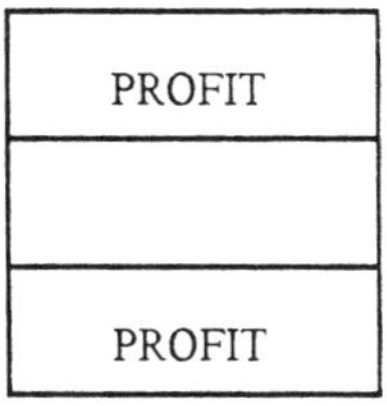	0.152 (2.048)
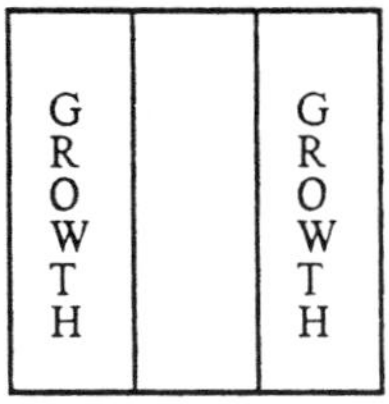	0.394 (2.042)	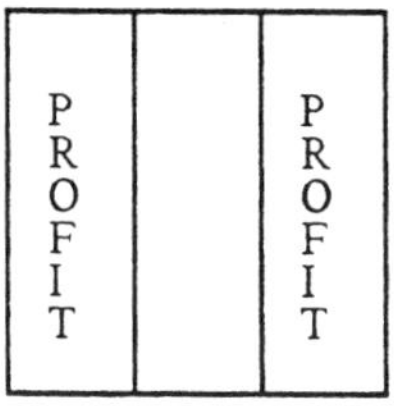	0.234 (2.042)
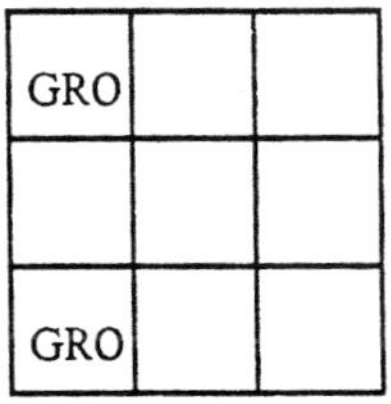	4.423 * (2.306)	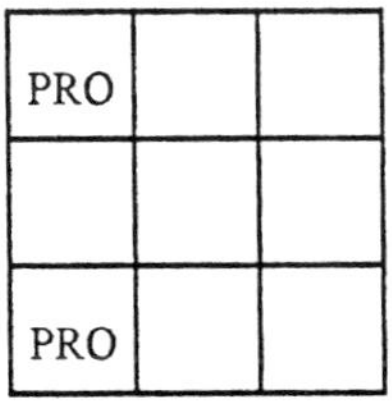	1.091 (2.306)

Table V-19 (Continued)

Subgroups	Computed (Critical) T-values	Subgroups	Computed (Critical) T-values
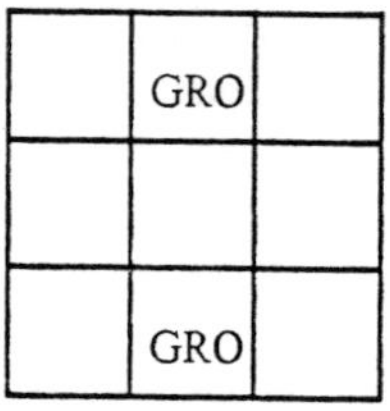	0.461 (2.160)	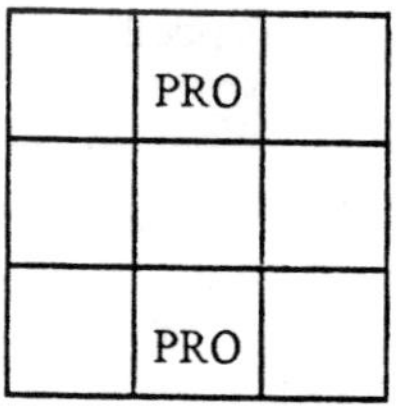	0.653 (2.160)
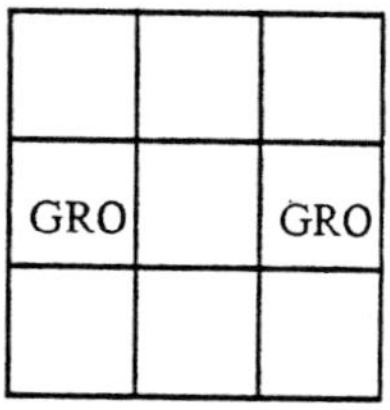	0.378 (2.101)	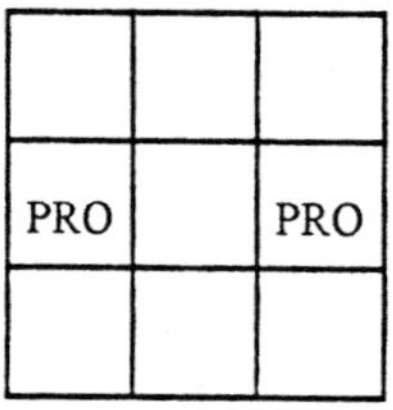	0.778 (2.101)
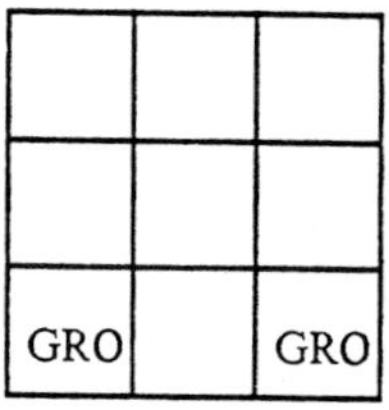	2.660 * (2.262)	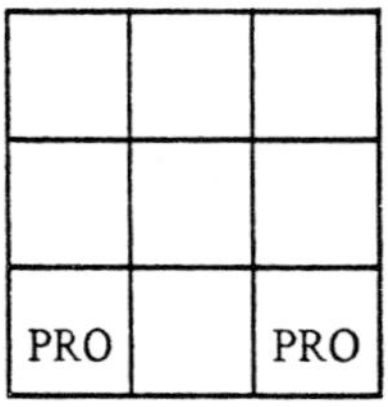	0.472 (2.262)

*The two sample means are significantly different from each other at the five percent level.

**The two sample means are significantly different from each other at the ten percent level.

CHAPTER VI

SUMMARY AND CONCLUSIONS

Summary

The United States Banking System, composed of a large number of independent banks, has provided a smoothly functioning banking service over the years. Nevertheless, economic changes during the last two decades have caused a decline in the profits of commercial banks. This development has been the source of much concern among bankers because of the important role of profits in the industry; some in fact consider adequate profits to be a precondition for the continued existence of the banking industry in its present form. The decline in profits is causing increased competition and is prompting bank executives to look for new and better techniques of management.

During the 1960's, studies suggested that profit planning techniques and long range planning could be applied successfully in commercial banks. These techniques were viewed as a possible solution to the problem that declining profits represent for the banking industry and the economy as a whole.

The awareness of this problem and a general paucity of long range planning literature in the field of banking led to the formulation of a set of hypotheses. These hypotheses were tested in this study to determine whether the success of a bank is correlated with the extent of long range planning efforts undertaken by the bank. Success in the study is represented by growth and profit trends experienced by the responding banks during the period from 1970 to 1974.

The general belief among businessmen is that a well-managed firm (bank) does not haphazardly achieve a certain profit level, but that profits are a result of extensive planning efforts. If this premise is true, long range planning efforts undertaken by banks should influence growth and profit trends favorably. A further objective of the study, therefore, was to collect data on the extent to which commercial banks engage in long range planning.

To establish the proper framework for the study, United States banking and its environment are discussed in Chapter II. The recent history of Financial Intermediaries and banking is briefly traced and discussed. A section on the Dual Banking System, a uniquely American feature, presents information on Federal and State regulations, the Federal Reserve System, the FDIC, bank-branching, mergers, and bank holding-companies. Salient features of banking environment, Fractional

Reserve System, economic developments, competition, changes in technology are also described.

Deposit and loan functions, the largest contributors to profit in commercial banks, are used as surrogates for the measurement of growth and profit trends in banks. In selecting the appropriate data-base for the study, uniformity of data and feasibility of collection were considered to be most important. Among the possible data-bases, the Functional Cost Analysis program (FCA) of the Federal Reserve System is the only data-bank that provides consistently uniform data for a large number of banks.

Chapter III contains a statement of the purpose of the Program as well as information on background and present use. Discussions of the data-base, the fund concept used in the Program, the structure of the annually published reports and a description of the participants follow. Fund Management and Fund Concepts used in the banking industry are also presented. A critical evaluation of advantages and disadvantages of the Program as management tool and data-base for this study conclude the chapter.

The methodology used in the study is considered in detail in Chapter IV. Questionnaires serve as the data-gathering device for this research project. The development of the instrument includes a sequence of steps, ranging from informal discussions with bankers and researchers to a formal pre-test. Under the sponsorship of the Bank Administration Institute, the questionnaire was mailed to member banks of the 7th Federal Reserve Bank district. All banks selected for this study are also participants in the FCA Program.

Sections of the questionnaire dealing specifically with long range planning aspects are used to compute a "long range planning score" for each bank. Participants are classified according to the computed "long range planning score" and bank size. Means for growth and profit trends for each research-partition are calculated. The Analysis of Variance procedure was selected to test the hypotheses formulated for the project. Chapter IV concludes with discussions of the procedures used for the long range planning data analysis, frequency tabulation of answers and crosstabulation tables.

Data relating to growth and profit are used to test the hypotheses designed to examine the following areas of relationships:

1. Bank size and extent of long range planning efforts undertaken

2. Bank size and trends for growth and profit

3. Extent of long range planning and trends for growth and profit

4. Extent of long range planning, bank size, and trends for growth and profit.

Data collected are also used to determine the extent to which commercial banks engage in long range planning activities.

Chapter V presents the analysis of empirical data gathered. The rationale of the Analysis of Variance procedure is illustrated by examining the first hypothesis of the study. Analysis of Variance tables for all seventeen hypotheses and a summary of the test results are presented. The chapter also includes a summary of t-test results.

The following sections summarize the findings of this research study and present interpretations of the results. A section on suggested future research concludes the chapter.

Conclusions

LRP and Trends for Growth and Profit

The main objectives of this study are: a) to ascertain whether there is a correlation between long range planning and growth trends and long range planning and profit trends; b) to examine the impact bank size might have on the extent of long range planning undertaken by a bank and on growth and profit trends.

The hypotheses discussed earlier were based on the assumption that both the extent of long range planning efforts a bank undertakes and bank size itself may be important factors influencing success in commercial banks. These hypotheses were tested for statistically significant differences in Chapter V. Table V-18 summarizes the test results and indicates which hypotheses were accepted or rejected.

The seventeen hypotheses were designed to examine the following specific areas of relationship:

1. Bank size and extent of long range planning efforts undertaken

2. Bank size and trends for growth and profit

3. Extent of long range planning and trends for growth and profit

4. Extent of long range planning, bank size and trends for growth and profit.

The evidence obtained from studying the relationship between bank size and the extent of long range planning effort undertaken by banks indicates that bank size does not seem to be a determining factor of the extent of long range planning efforts undertaken by banks. The test results reveal a relationship that is not statistically significant at the 5% level.

The second set of hypotheses examines the relationship between bank size and trends for growth and profit. Test results show that bank size is an important variable affecting growth in commercial banks. Small banks experienced the highest average growth rates during the time period of the study. Large banks had growth rates that were substantially smaller than those of small banks but slightly higher than those experienced by medium banks.

The data collected do not permit inferences as to why small banks experienced higher growth rates than large and medium sized banks. A possible explanation is that small banks operate in less saturated markets that permit more expansion than markets served by large and medium banks.

While bank size seems to affect growth trends in commercial banks included in this study, a discernible impact on profit cannot be gleaned from the test results. In some instances, profits might be subject to variables that negate the impact of size. For example, banks could follow a policy of maintaining at least minimum growth rates even at the cost of lower profit rates. No empirical evidence, however, is available to support this explanation. Although profits for individual banks varied widely, the dispersion "within groups" was so large in relation to the differences "among groups" that the analysis of variance-test resulted in an insignificant F-ratio. Comparisons of growth and profit trends of large banks to growth and profit trends of small banks produced similar results. Growth trends for large banks are significantly different from growth trends for small banks at the 10% level of significance. No significant difference exists between profit trends for large and small banks.

Testing the relationship of the extent of long range planning effort undertaken and trends for growth and profit revealed no statistically significant correlation between long range planning effort on one side and growth or profit trends on the other side. Although statistically not significant, the data analysis revealed that the group of banks engaging to a low extent in long range planning, experienced the lowest average increase in growth during the test period. As above, the dispersion of results "within groups" was so large in relation to the dispersion "among groups" that the resulting F-ratio was statistically insignificant at the 5% level.

The last set of hypotheses tests relationships of long range planning extent, bank size, and trends for growth and profit. Analysis results reveal statistically significant differences only in growth trends experienced by high long range planning banks of different sizes (large, medium, and small). Small banks (engaging to a high extent in long range planning) experienced the largest average increases in growth. Medium banks (engaging to a high extent in long range planning) experienced slightly larger average increases in growth than large banks. The data collected indicate that small banks (engaging to a high degree in long range planning) also experienced the largest average increases in profits, followed by medium and finally large banks. The tests for profit trends again were statistically insignificant at the 5% level.

Comparisons of large to small banks and banks engaging to a high extent in long range planning to banks engaging to a low extent in long range planning produced some additional significant findings. First, the previously discussed importance of bank size on growth trends is confirmed. Second, in small banks the extent of long range planning effort undertaken is affecting growth trends. Small banks engaging to a high extent in long range planning experience significantly higher growth rates than small banks engaging in a low extent in long range planning. As discussed earlier (refer to Table V-18) no further significant relationships were detected through the testing.

The preponderance of the evidence obtained in studying the relationship between bank size, extent of long range planning efforts undertaken, and trends for growth and profit leads to the conclusion that bank size is an important variable affecting growth trends in commercial banks. Test results suggest that the extent of long range planning efforts undertaken influences growth trends. The influence exerted by the extent of long range planning efforts, however, does not seem to be as strong as the impact of size. Significant differences in growth rate changes can be observed in banks of different sizes engaging in long range planning to a high extent and small banks engaging in long range planning to a high and to a low extent.

No explanation supported by empirical evidence is provided by the study to account for the test results concerning the impact long range planning and size may have on profit. As explained earlier, one possible explanation is the existence of variables not considered in this research design that have an impact on profit that negates or counteracts any influence size or extent of long range planning may have.

Any inferences from these conclusions have to be made in view of the limitations set forth earlier (refer to Chapters I and IV). From the large number of diversified products and services that a bank, under normal conditions, offers customers, only the main "contributor" to overall bank profit was used as surrogate for growth and profit trends. As data base for the measures used served Functional Cost Analysis reports. In addition, it should be noted that the fruits of long range planning efforts undertaken may not appear until long range planning has been practiced by the bank for a number of years. With repeated use, long range planning can undoubtedly become more refined. The application might become more intense and be extended to cover a wider sphere of the bank's business. If trends for growth and profit are observed over a longer time period, that is, if long range planning is put to work over an extended time horizon, the test results may well be different.

Long Range Planning Practice in Commercial Banks

As reported previously, several studies during the 1960's (notably Olson and Hegazy) suggested that profit planning and long range planning could also be applied in commercial banks. The success of commercial banks is reported to be a necessity for their survival. Success, rcpresented to a large measure by profit and growth, is not achieved haphazardly. On the contrary, profits are a result of extensive planning efforts, which to be meaningful must be achieved in view of all considerations within the firm.

Recognizing the importance of success (profit and growth) and noting the general paucity of long range planning literature for commercial banks led to the formulation of an additional objective for this study: to determine to what extent commercial banks use long range planning as a management tool.

The surveyed banks are grouped according to size: large banks (1/5 of all banks), medium and small banks (2/5 each). Three quarters of the banks have a national charter and one quarter a state charter. Roughly one half of the banks have trading-areas with populations of between 100,000 to 500,000. Only 16% of the banks have trading-areas of less than 25,000 people. The remaining 1/3 of all respondents falls between 25,000 to 100,000 people.

Locally dominant industries do not affect the majority of the banks. Market dominance is quite concentrated. A little less than half of all the banks report very strong control of the local market. The strongest concentration of market share occurs among banks whose dependency on one locally dominant industry is low. Banks which engage in long range planning to a high and moderate extent control larger shares of their local markets than banks that do little long range planning.

The review of the literature and discussions with bankers revealed that the industry is very much concerned with maintaining an adequate profit performance. Profits are the results of extensive planning efforts, both short and long range, and are considered necessary to meet the expectations of shareholders for dividends and continued growth. Firms subject to levels of profit consistently less than adequate may not survive. This concern for profit is confirmed by the survey. More than two thirds of the banks consider adequate profits as their overriding goal. Customer satisfaction is reported as second most important goal, followed by growth. Staff development takes on fourth place and community service is considered least important.

The majority of banks consider a three year planning horizon for long range planning in commercial banks as most practical and desirable. Balance Sheet and Income projections (both short term, up to one year, and long term, beyond one year) are prepared by most banks. The preparation of the Statement of Sources and Uses of Funds (Statement of Changes in Financial Position), however, has not yet found the same acceptance.

Many banks prepare detailed overall and departmentalized profit plans. The responsibility for long range planning rests largely with top management, possibly because long range planning is still a rather recent development in commercial banks (approximately half of the surveyed banks began long range planning during or before 1972). Most long range plans are formalized (in writing).

Among the more important goals included in long range planning efforts are forecasts for corporate objectives (strategic plans), capital funds, fixed assets, investments, volume of deposits (often also by deposit category), and volume of loans (also by loan category). Forecasts for manpower planning and control, product planning (new services and improvements, etc.), organizational structure and development planning, bank-image advertising and promotion, staff training, product advertising and promotion, market share planning and competitor action command less attention.

Very few banks enlist the expertise of outside consultants in making long range plans. Instead, they rely extensively on a variety of sources of information: Government agencies, economists, magazines (e.g., *Fortune*) and newspaper reports (e.g., *Wall Street Journal*). Attempts are made to identify developments in the following areas: economic trends, population trends, technological breakthroughs, and growth of the money supply, to name a few of the more important ones.

Of the planning techniques used by bankers, predictions on recurring business cycles are most favored. Many small and medium banks rely heavily on forecasts made by correspondent banks. Rather then making comprehensive studies of the economy, many bankers look for and rely on the prediction of key elements. Attempts to predict Federal Authorities' policies that might affect interest rates also rank high in planning activities. This is not surprising because changes in interest rates have an immediate impact on profit.

Naive forecasts, basing future plans on the assumption of the continuation of current business conditions, are used to some extent by small and medium banks. Reliance on patterns of relationship of various economic activities and use of "lead series" are less frequently encountered as planning approaches. Cost factors and lack of familiarity with available tools seem to be the major reasons why only a few banks either have an economist participating in forecasting or use computers and econometric models in long range planning.

Almost all long range plans are prepared on an annual basis. Updates are sometimes made more frequently. Top management realizes the importance of long range planning and generally provides strong support.

Avoidance of a decline in profits is cited as the most compelling reason for long range planning. This demonstrates again how important a role profits play in commercial banking. Increased size and complexity of business and increased competition, both influencing profit indirectly, are also mentioned as important reasons for long range planning. Banks not currently engaging in long range planning cited most frequently staffing problems and the lack of top management support as reasons for their failure to make long range forecasts.

The survey results clearly reveal that a general awareness of the importance of long range planning is shared by many bankers. A variety of planning techniques are used today by banks of all sizes, although the use of some of the more "sophisticated" approaches to long range planning is still very restricted. Lack of understanding and, for small and medium banks, cost and staffing problems, seem to be mainly responsible for this.

Overall, one can conclude that compared to the period of the mid 1960's, when long range planning was first proposed for use in commercial banks, the industry has made considerable progress in this respect.

General Inference

A general inference can also be drawn from the study: that long range planning in banks has great future potential. The use of long range planning in banking is a fairly new development. Nevertheless, the results of this study have shown that long range planning is affecting growth in banks. The study further revealed that long range planning has become more widespread in its application in commercial banks as compared to a decade ago.

Because long range planning is relatively new to banking, it is possible that banks have not yet mastered the process. The majority of bankers participating in this study, however, have come to realize that the question is not whether or not, or when, a bank should engage in long range planning, but rather to what extent. Without any doubt, long range planning can play an important role in anticipating future developments, making early decisions, and translating a changing environment into profitable banking operations.

Declining interest margins, exploding operating expenses, increased complexity of business operations, and keener competition are some of the most compelling reasons for the adoption of long range planning. In the long run the very survival of the industry is at stake.

Suggested Future Research

Some further avenues for research which can supplement the work covered in this study are presented below. Other questions not discussed in this study might be of equal interest. To treat all areas of interest is, however, not possible in the framework of a research project.

Other Federal Reserve Districts

It would be worthwhile to perform the analyses and tests described in this research project in the remaining (eleven) Federal Reserve districts. Comparisons of the results will reveal whether findings of this study apply to some or all Federal Reserve districts. Differences in size of district in terms of geographical area and volume of business may exercise influences that lead to different results.

Time Period

Only a short time was covered in the study. Would the effects uncovered hold true over longer spans, or would some of them weaken and others arise to take their place? It would be useful to replicate the study in the 7th Federal Reserve district several years from now to determine whether the use of long range planning has increased and to assess the impact a prolonged application of long range planning efforts has on growth and profit trends.

Other Segments of Banking Operations

It would be possible to replicate the study by focusing on other important segments of a bank's operations (e.g., investments, trust departments) to determine the degree to which they are subject to long range forecasts.

Other Industries

The study design could be modified to make it suitable for determining the impact of long range planning in other industries, and to make comparisons among industries, including banking.

Commercial Banks in Other Countries

The methods of this study could be used to determinc whether compatible data-bases exist in other countries. Analyses and tests described in this study could be performed. Comparisons of the results will reveal whether findings of this study differ from those in other countries. Also, long range planning practices in the United States could be compared with those abroad to determine whether these differences (e.g., cultural, economic, legal) might influence growth and profit trends.

The results of these suggested studies, combined with the results of the present study, should make a significant contribution to the determination of the role long range planning plays in successfully managing a commercial bank, or for that matter, any firm. The full benefit of studies in managerial accounting utilization in commercial banks can be realized over extended time periods if continued improvements and developments are accepted and implemented by bank management.

APPENDIX A

QUESTIONNAIRE AND COVER LETTER

Questionnaire

All information furnished will be kept strictly confidential and will be used only in aggregation in our analysis. We will share the results of our study with you.

Instructions: Please check the appropriate box(es) for yes-answers, leave blank for no-answers or when not applicable, and fill in the blank space where required. For additional comments or information use the space provided on the last page of this questionnaire.

1. Does your Bank

☐ a. Hold a National Charter?
☐ b. Hold a State Charter?
☐ c. Have the corporate form of a one-bank holding company?
☐ d. Have the corporate form of a multi-bank holding company?
☐ e. Have domestic branches?
☐ f. Have international branches?

2. If your Bank has branches, indicate the *number* by type of operation (excluding the main-office) in the space provided.

_______a. Full Service
_______b. Limited Service
_______c. Paying and Receiving Stations
_______d. Total branches (equals a,b,c)

3. The trading area of your Bank (incl. branches) has a population of:

☐ a. Under 25,000 ☐ b. 25,000 to 100,000
☐ c. 100,000 to 500,000 ☐ d. Over 500,000

4. The service area of your Bank is: (check more than one, if applicable)

☐ a. Rural ☐ b. Suburban ☐ c. Urban ☐ d. National

5. To what degree is your Bank's service area economically dependent on the "fortunes" of one dominant industry?

☐ a. High ☐ b. Moderate ☐ c. Low

6. How long has the chief-executive of your Bank held his current position?

☐ a. 0 to 4 years ☐ b. 4 to 10 years ☐ c. More than 10 years

7. What is your overall share of the "local Banking Market?"

☐ a. 0 to 10% ☐ b. 10 to 25% ☐ c. 25 to 40% ☐ d. More than 40%

8. What importance does your Bank attach to the following goals? First evaluate the goals in terms of their importance to you by checking the appropriate box (H=High, M=Moderate, L=Low) and second, rank the goals in accordance to the priority you assign to them.

H	M	L	Goal	Rank
☐	☐	☐	a. Adequate profits	1._____
☐	☐	☐	b. Growth	2._____
☐	☐	☐	c. Customer Satisfaction	3._____
☐	☐	☐	d. Community Service	4._____
☐	☐	☐	e. Staff Development	5._____
☐	☐	☐	f. Other, please list____________________	

9. What planning horizon do you consider as reasonable and manageable for banks in general?

☐ a. Up to 1 year ☐ b. Up to 2 years ☐ c. Up to 3 years
☐ d. Up to 4 years ☐ e. More than 4 years

10. For a yes-answer check the appropriate box.

☐ a. Do you prepare written budgets covering up to one year?
Do your one-year budgets include forecasts of pro-forma:
☐ b. Balance Sheet ☐ c. Income Statement
☐ d. Statement of Sources and Uses of Funds
☐ e. Do you establish work-standards for your personnel (e.g. guidelines concerning processing-time of loans)?

☐ f. Do you have a profit planning program (e.g. do you plan overall profit and then develop profit-contributions expected from each functional area, department, or branch)?

☐ g. Do you engage in *any* Long Range Planning (=LRP), e.g., plans and forecasts that *cover more than one year*?

11. Who is responsible for LRP in your Bank?

☐ a. A corporate planning department
☐ b. All, or selected members of top-management
☐ c. Functional areas, departments, or branches

A combination of:
☐ d. (a) and (b) ☐ e. (a) and (c) ☐ f. (a), (b), and (c)
☐ g. Other, please list

12. When did your Bank start with LRP?

☐ a. During 1975 ☐ b. During 1974 ☐ c. During 1973
☐ d. During 1972 ☐ e. During 1971 ☐ f. During 1970
☐ g. Before 1970

13. Which of the following pro-forma statements are included in your LRP?

☐ a. Balance Sheet ☐ b. Income Statement
☐ c. Statement of Sources and Uses of Funds.

14. Is most of your LRP:

☐ a. Formalized (in writing)? ☐ b. Discussed orally only?

15. Which of the following are included in your LRP and how far into the future are they projected?

Years
_______ a. Corporate objectives (e.g. strategic plans)
_______ b. Capital funds
_______ c. Fixed Assets
_______ d. Investments
_______ e. Volume of deposits
_______ f. Volume of deposits by deposit category
_______ g. Volume of loans

_______h. Volume of loans by loan category
_______i. Manpower planning and control
_______j. Staff training
_______k. Product planning (new services and improvements, etc.)
_______l. Product advertising and promotion
_______m. Bank-image advertising and promotion
_______n. Organizational structure and development planning
_______o. Interaction between functional areas, departments and/or branches
_______p. Competitor action
_______q. Market share planning
_______r. Other, please list_______________

16. Does your information system permit

☐ a. The monitoring of your LRP efforts?
☐ b. To calculate interest rates and loan yields?

17. Have you enlisted the expertise of any of the following outside consultants to assist you in the LRP activities?

☐ a. Research firms
☐ b. Consulting firms (incl. CPA's)
☐ c. Independent Professionals
☐ d. Other, please list_______

18. Which of the following is your LRP attempting to identify.

☐ a. Population trends
☐ b. Social currents
☐ c. Political developments
☐ d. Labor-Management relations
☐ e. Personal incomes
☐ f. Technological breakthroughs
☐ g. Economic trends
☐ h. Growth of money supply
☐ i. Other, please list_______________

19. Which of the following do you consult in making forecasts?

☐ a. Magazine (e.g., *Fortune, Economist, Newsweek*)
☐ b. Government Agencies (e.g., Federal Reserve Bank, Commerce Department)
☐ c. Business Associations (e.g., Dun & Bradstreet)
☐ d. Experts on future business conditions (e.g., economists)
☐ e. Newspaper reports (e.g., *Wallstreet Journal, New York Times*)
☐ f. Other, please list_______________

20. Do you:

- ☐ a. Base your prediction of future activities on the assumption of the continuation of current business conditions?
- ☐ b. Survey present plans of industrial leaders in key positions in industry to uncover and predict what will happen between now and the time these plans are completed and how these developments might affect your bank now and then?
- ☐ c. Rely on forecasts made by your correspondent banks?
- ☐ d. Use "lead series" (e.g., economic indicators used by Commerce and Labor Department) developed from past movements in economic activities to predict future developments?
- ☐ e. Rely on patterns of relationship of various economic activities (e.g., if it is possible to predict important segments, it may be possible to predict the whole structure by relying on past relationships)?
- ☐ f. Look for recurring business cycles, applicable to your bank, and helpful in LRP?
- ☐ g. Look for, and rely on key elements, rather than making comprehensive studies of the entire economy?
- ☐ h. Predict Federal Authorities' policies that might affect interest rates?
- ☐ i. Have an economist on the staff who participates in forecasting?
- ☐ j. Use a computer in any phase of your LRP? Please describe briefly on the last page how you use the computer.
- ☐ k. Use econometric models in your LRP? Please describe briefly on the last page the models you use.
- ☐ 1. Compare a list of all favorable factors with a list of all unfavorable factors in making predictions?

21. How frequently are your Long-Range Plans prepared?

☐ a. Quarterly ☐ b. Semi-annually ☐ c. Annually

22. How frequently are your Long-Range Plans up-dated?

☐ a. Monthly ☐ b. Quarterly ☐ c. Semi-annually
☐ d. Annually ☐ e. Other, please list________________

23. To what degree is top management supporting LRP?

☐ a. Very strongly ☐ b. Strongly ☐ c. Occasionally

24. Which of the following are the important reasons for your choosing to engage in LRP? (You may check more than one).

- ☐ a. Increased competition ☐ b. To avoid decline in profits
- ☐ c. Decreased Interest margin
- ☐ d. Increased size and complexity of business
- ☐ e. Increased variety and number of services offered
- ☐ f. Chief-executive encourages LRP
- ☐ g. Other, please list________________________

25. Which of the following are the important reasons for your choosing *not to engage* in LRP? (You may check more than one).

- ☐ a. Lack of proven success. ☐ b. Too time-consuming
- ☐ c. Not accurate enough ☐ d. Lack of planning guides
- ☐ e. Staffing problems ☐ f. No support by top management
- ☐ g. Environmental conditions are not predictable
- ☐ h. The necessary information is not available or quantifiable
- ☐ i. Other, please list________________________

26. From the data that you supply to the Federal Reserve Bank for the annual compilation of the FUNCTIONAL COST ANALYSIS report, please provide us with the following information:

	1974	1973	1972	1971	1970
AVERAGE DEPOSITS FCA report page 3 Line 26 Deposits (Total)	$_____	$_____	$_____	$_____	$_____
PORTFOLIO, LOANS AND INVESTMENTS FCA report page 5 Line 37 Memo- Net Yield after Cost of Cash	$_____	$_____	$_____	$_____	$_____

Comment to question 20j.
Use of the computer in LRP:

Comment to question 20k.
Use of econometric models in LRP:

Other comments:

THANK YOU VERY MUCH FOR YOUR COOPERATION.

BANK ADMINISTRATION INSTITUTE
PARK RIDGE, ILLINOIS 60068 PHONE 312-775-5344

RONALD G. BURKE
EXECUTIVE VICE PRESIDENT

June 2, 1976

Dear BAI Member:

One of the many services of BAI is locating and encouraging young men who are candidates for doctor's degrees, and whose studies are in areas of specific interest to BAI's member banks. Assistance is given in many forms, one of which is to help these candidates obtain information that they think will be of value in preparing their dissertations.

Hans Klein is a doctoral candidate at the University of Kentucky in Lexington. He has worked in top management positions in banks and as Controller for several Multi-National companies. He was actively involved in planning and has done research in this area.

We feel that Hans Klein's project, Long-Range Planning in Commercial Banks, is of considerable interest to the banking industry and we are, therefore, happy to assist. We have selected a representative list of banks and we are asking them to cooperate in this study.

Will you please invest 15 minutes of your time and supply the information requested in the questionnaire. Please return your answer at the earliest convenience directly to

Hans E. Klein
College of Business and Economics
University of Kentucky
Lexington, Kentucky 40506

using the self-addressed envelope provided.

Thank you for helping.

Sincerely,

Ronald G. Burke
President

RGB:jf

APPENDIX B

DEFINITIONS

Some key-terms used in connection with this study are defined in this section.

1. *Long range planning* in the context of this study encompasses *all* planning activities that exceed a time horizon of one year. Capital-budgeting, although an important aspect of long range planning, is only *one* facet of long range planning. Long range planning is a process that includes essentially the same factors considered in the development of the short range plan (with which it is integrated), although the emphasis is somewhat different. The planning horizon is longer (more than one year), the amount of detail and degree of accuracy is less (by design), and predicting, assessing and developing significant responses to the future is emphasized.

The time horizon that the bank chooses for planning is influenced primarily by the extent, nature, duration and rapidity of change the bank expects to face, and its ability to predict the direction and degree of change; the predicted life of major investments of time and money, the time required to implement major decisions; and the time required to react to environmental changes. The initial step of most long range planning procedures is the development of the bank's strategic objectives by top management and the managers in charge of major functions and departments or branches.

The forecast of strategic objectives will indicate the programs and services to be offered, the number of banking locations, and the people and equipment needed. Plans will be developed for results and achievements, for example, for the next five years without developing detailed plans for implementation. Historical, present, and future-oriented data is provided by other specialists and external sources.

During this part of the process, overall corporate objectives are defined in such terms as earnings growth, return on investment, share of market, and desired loan and deposit growth rates; and planning guidelines are established. These guidelines may take the form of economic forecasts, forecasts of competitor action and policy statements.

Having prepared the bank's strategic objectives and planning guidelines, the officers begin the development of plans for major activities. They examine the various alternatives available for achieving them, evaluate the probable costs and results, and alter the original goals and objectives accordingly when this is necessary. Definitions of responsibility for achievement may be clarified and formalized at this stage if they are not self-evident. Staff assistance is given to management as the specialist acts to provide information; to fit plans together; and to review, question, and eventually integrate the separate plans, developed by the officers, into a single corporate plan.

Management then reviews the corporate plan, considering it in light of the original or amended objectives. If these are not satisfied by the initial plan, they may be changed, other measures to achieve them may be evaluated, or the plans or planning assumptions may be revised. In this way an interactive planning cycle is developed. This process continues until management is satisfied that workable plans have been developed to reach reasonable objectives.[109]

The similarity to short term planning is quite apparent. In most respects the approach is the same. Variations primarily involve differences in accuracy and detail, greater orientation toward planning rather than control, and greater awareness of environmental changes. Officials and employees below the level of top management participate proportionately less in LRP activities.

2. *The extent of long range planning* undertaken by the bank was determined through the use of interviews and the questionnaire shown in Appendix A. Questions 1, 2, 3, 4, 5, 6, 7, 8, 9, 11, 12, 14, 18, 25 are designed to provide descriptive data of the banks; question 26 asks for the data necessary to determine bank size, growth trends and profit trends, as used in this study. The remaining questions, 10, 13, 15, 16, 17, 19, 20, 21, 22, 23, 24, are designed to permit the classification of the responding banks according to the extent of their long range planning activities into three classes, high long range planning, moderate long range planning, and low long range planning.

The underlying criteria for the formulation of the questions used to determine the degree of long range planning were:

— the completeness of the planning process, including comprehensiveness of input and output of information;
— time horizon employed;
— frequency of revisions and up-date of plans;
— degree of detail, and
— degree of flexibility.

A "pro forma profile" of a high, moderate, and low long range planning bank is included in Appendix C. This profile was developed before the data was actually collected and draws on the banking literature as well as the many discussion and interviews conducted during the development of the study. (Refer to earlier discussion.)

The definition of the "extent of long range planning," in addition to being based on the above mentioned criteria, is anchored in the definition of long range planning in commercial banks as discussed under No. 1 in this section. The "Analysis of Long Range Planning Questions" presented in Appendix D links the definition of long range planning in commercial banks with the above mentioned questions used to classify the banks into the three classes of extent of long range planning.

3. *Bank size* was determined by total average deposits of each participating bank during the year 1970. Responding banks were partitioned into the following three groups:

1. Banks with total deposits of more than $200 million (class A)

2. Banks with total deposits from $50 million to $200 million (class B)

3. Banks with total deposits of up to $50 million (class C).

Classifying the participating banks by deposit size permits more meaningful comparisons among banks. The three size classes used are the same as those used by the Functional Cost Analysis program and thus will not only allow a comparison of the results of this research with Functional Cost Analysis reports, but also better analysis, and if desired, follow-up studies. Data for average deposits were supplied by the responding banks by answering question No. 26 of the questionnaire and represent the data used for the Functional Cost Analysis report prepared by the bank on an annual basis.

4. *Growth,* as used in this study, is measured by computing the percentage changes (increases or decreases) of average total deposits of the banks, included in the sample for the years 1970-1974. Data on average deposits were collected as explained under No. 3 above. Average deposit figures for each bank are those used by the bank in preparing the annual Functional Cost Analysis report. Because of the uniform procedures used by all banks that participate in the Functional Cost Analysis program, comparability among and within banks and from year to year is assured.

5. *Profit,* as used in this study, refers to the Net Yield after Cost of Cash, as defined and used in the Functional Cost Analysis program. The Net Yield is computed by combining the "Net Yield after Cost of Money" for all classes of loans, the "Net Yield after Cost of Money" for investments, and the "Cash and Due from Banks" balance. The last item is deducted since the "Cash and Due from Banks" balance represents idle funds and, therefore, no income is available to offset the deduction of the Cost of Money. The necessary data were collected through the questionnaire as explained under No. 3 above. (For a detailed description of the exact computation and examples, refer to the "Explanatory Guide to the Calculations and Techniques employed in the Functional Cost Analysis Report," especially the section on page 40.)[110]

6. *The Bank Administration Institute* is a non-profit organization whose broad goals are to help bank administrators achieve high levels of professional effectiveness and to help solve significant banking problems. These goals are pursued through programs of research and development, education, and technical assistance. Founded in 1924, the Institute is today the largest technical banking association in the world. The Institute serves more than 9,000 member banks (commercial banks) through 270 chapters in the United States, Puerto Rico, and the Philippines with comprehensive programs in accounting, administration, auditing, security, control, EDP, education, personnel administration, operations, planning, research, taxes, and trusts. The Bank Administration publishes a wide variety of books, manuals, surveys, bulletins, and reports, as well as a monthly magazine and a quarterly research journal.

The Institute is governed by a Board of Directors with the President acting as Chairman. The responsibility for management of the Institute's activities, within a framework of policies established by the Board, rests with the Executive Director, who is assited by a headquarter staff located in Park Ridge, Illinois.

7. *Federal Reserve System.* In 1913, Congress established the Federal Reserve System, composed of twelve Federal Reserve Banks with the power to issue Federal Reserve Notes, hold reserves of member banks, and lend to member banks to meet heavy demands on them for credit or deposit withdrawals. A Federal Reserve Board was established in Washington with powers of the system shared between the Reserve Banks and the Board. Over the years, during the 1920's and especially in the 1930's, the Federal Reserve System has taken on additional

responsibilities: managing the nation's money supply, setting monetary policy, stabilizing the economy.

8. *Federal Deposit Insurance Corporation (FDIC).* The Banking Act of 1933 established the Federal Deposit Insurance Corporation. The FDIC is regarded as one of the principal reforms arising from the Depression. Virtually all commercial banks and most mutual savings banks are members of the FDIC. Creation of the Federal Reserve Banks in 1913 was largely an effort to improve the safety of banks. The creation of the FDIC has a major impact in calming fears about smaller banks.

In return for the insurance of its accounts, a bank pays an annual fee of 0.2 percent of the insured deposits and submits to annual examinations. The FDIC imposes certain restrictions on the bank's asset portfolio. Deposits are insured only up to a set limit, presently $20,000 per account. The FDIC tends to make small banks competitively stronger than they otherwise would be.

9. *SPSS (Statistical Package for the Social Sciences)* is an integrated system of computer programs designed for the analysis of social science data. The system allows the user considerable flexibility in creating independent data sets and in performing several different types of analysis on any of the data sets in a single run. In addition to the usual descriptive statistics, simple frequency distributions, and cross-tabulations, SPSS contains procedures for simple correlation (for both ordinal and interval data), partial correlation, one-way and n-way analysis variance (including multiple classification analysis tables), multiple regression, discriminant analysis, scatter diagrams, factor analysis, canonical correlations, and Guttman Scaling.

The data management facilities can be used to modify a file of data permanently and can also be used in conjunction with any of the statistical procedures. The facilities enable the user to generate new variables which are mathematical and/or logical combinations of existing variables, to recode variables, and to sample, select, or weight specified cases. Furthermore, the user can add to or alter the data cases or the data-descriptional information in the file, such as labels, missing value codes, etc. The user can perform an analysis through the use of natural language control statements.[111]

APPENDIX C

PRO FORMA COMPUTATION OF SCORES FOR LRP-CLASSIFICATION

Note: Banks with high-LRP-efforts might answer all or some of the questions appearing in the "H-column." Banks with moderate-LRP-efforts might answer all or some of the questions in the M-column. Banks with low-LRP-efforts might answer all or some of the questions appearing in the L-column. If more than one question is listed on any one line, the researcher expects that the bank will answer one of the questions listed with *yes*.

H	M	L
9c,d,e	9b	9a
10a	10a	10a
10b	10b	
10d	10d	
10e		
10f	10f	
10g	10g	
13a,c,d,e,f	13b,c	
15a	15a	
15b	15b	
15c		
16a	16a	16b
17a	17a	
17b	17b	17b
17c	17c	17c
17d	17d	
17e	17e	
17f		
17g	17g	
17h		
17i	17i	17i
17j	17j	
17k		
17l		
17m		

	H	M	L
	17n	17n	
	17o		
	18a	18a	
	18b	18b	18b
	19a		
	19b	19b	19b
	19c		
	20a		
	20b		
	20c		
	20d	20d	
	20e		
	20f	20f	
	20g	20g	
	20h	20h	20h
	21a		
	21b	21b	21b
	21c	21c	
	21d		
	21e	21e	
			22a
	22b		
		22c	22c
	22d		
	22e	22e	
	22f		
		22g	
	22h	22h	
	22i		
	22j		
	22k	22k	
		22l	22l
	23a,b	23a,b	23c
	24a,b	24b,c	24c,d
Score	55	37	15

APPENDIX D

ANALYSIS OF LRP-QUESTIONS

Long Range Planning Defined	Questions
Long range planning is a process that considers essentially the same factors used in the	10a, b, c, d, e
development of the short-range plan, with which it is integrated, although the emphasis is some-	10g
what different. The planning horizon is longer, the amount of detail and degree of accuracy is	13a, b, c
less, and predicting, assessing and developing significant responses to the future is emphasized.	18a through 18i
The time horizon that the bank chooses for planning is influenced primarily by the extent, nature, duration and rapidity of change the bank	18a through 18i
expects to face and its ability to predict the direction and degree of change; the predicted life	15i, j, k, l, m, n, o
of major investments of time and money; the time required to implement major decisions; and the	15a
time required to react to environmental changes.	18a through 18i
The initial step of most LRP procedures is the development of the bank's strategic objectives	18g, 11
by top management and the managers in charge	10b, c, d, e, f
of major functions. The forecast for the strategic	15a through 15r
objectives will indicate the programs and services	10e, f
to be offered, the number of banking locations, and the people needed to provide them. Plans will be developed for results and achievements, e.g., for the next five years, without developing detailed plans for implementation. Historical, present and future-oriented data is provided by	17a, b, c, d
other specialists and external sources.	19a, b, c, d, e, f
During this part of the process, overall corporate objectives are defined in terms such as	15a, q
earnings growth, return on investments, share of market, and desired loan and deposit growth rates; and planning guidelines are established.	14a, b
These guidelines may take the form of economic	20d, 15a, p, q, 20a, b

Long Range Planning Defined	Questions
forecasts, forecasts of competitor action and policy statements.	20c through 201
Having prepared the bank's strategic objectives and planning guidelines, the officers	11
begin the development of plans for major activities. They examine the various alternatives	20a through 201
available for achieving these plans, evaluate the probable cost and results, and alter the original goals and objectives accordingly when this is	21
necessary. Definitions of responsibility for achievement may be clarified and formalized at this stage if they are not self-evident. Staff assistance is given to management as the specialist acts to provide information, to fit plans together,	17a, b, c, d
and to review, question and eventually integrate	22, 11
the separate plans developed by the officers into a single corporate plan.	15o
Management then reviews the corporate	11, 22
plan, considering it in light of the original or amended objectives. If these are not satisfied by the initial plan, they may be changed, other measures to achieve the objectives may be evaluated, or the plans or planning assumptions	20a through 201
may be revised. In this way an interactive planning cycle is developed. This process continues until management is satisfied that workable plans have been developed to reach reasonable objectives.	
The similarity to short-term planning is quite apparent. In most respects the approach is the same. Variations primarily involve differences in	13, 14, 15a through 15r
accuracy and detail, greater orientation toward planning rather than control, greater awareness of environmental changes. Officials and employees	10, 15
below the level of top management participate proportionately less in LRP activities.	11

APPENDIX E

GEOMETRIC MEAN

When questions concerning the average percentage rates of change over time arise, neither the mean, median nor mode is the appropriate average to use. The correct answers can be obtained through the use of the Geometric Mean.

The use of the Geometric Mean is illustrated by the following example: Consider the following sales figures for a company from 1960 through 1963:

	Sales
1960	$10,000,000
1961	8,000,000
1962	12,000,000
1963	15,000,000

What was the average percentage rate of change per year in sales? To answer this question, we must specify what we mean by the "average percentage rate of change per year." The most generally useful interpretation of this term is the constant percentage rate of change which, if applied each year would take us from the first to the last figure. Hence, in the above illustration, we would be interested in that constant yearly percentage rate of change which would be required to move from $10 million of sales in 1961 to $15 million in 1963. Neither the mean, median nor mode provides the correct answer to this question. The correct answer can be obtained through the Geometric Mean.[112]

The Geometric Mean, (G), of n numbers is defined as the n-th root of the product of n numbers

$$G = \sqrt[n]{x_1 \cdot x_2 \cdot \ \ldots \ \cdot x_n}$$

This definition can be contrasted to that of the arithmetic mean, (X), which is the sum of n numbers divided by n,

$$\overline{X} = \frac{\sum_{i}^{n} x}{n}$$

The Geometric Mean of n numbers is always equal to or less than the arithmetic mean. When all numbers are identical, the two averages are equal.

To facilitate computations, the compound interest formula (below) is often used as a substitute for the above formula for the Geometric Mean. This is possible because of the relationship between this average and compound interest. For further details refer to Morris Hamburg or any standard textbook on Statistical Analysis.[113]

$$G = \sqrt[n]{\frac{Pn}{Po}}$$

The Geometric Mean for the above example is 14.5%. It is important to keep in mind that the typicality of the computed average can only be judged in terms of the individual percentage rate of change. The annual rates of change for the above example were -20%, +50%, and +25%. Clearly, the 14.5% average rate of change is not typical of such widely fluctuating figures. On the other hand, if sales had gone from $10 million to $15 million at relatively constant annual rates, the computed average would bc a typical figure.

In interpreting an average, such as the 14.5% rate of change, it is important to note the effect of using only the terminal points, Po and Pn, of the time series. In dealing with economic data in which cycles appear, if the measurement of an average percentage rate of change is made by taking the first figure, Po, at the trough of a business cycle, while the last point, Pn, is taken at the peak of a cycle, clearly a greater average rate will tend to be obtained that if the two selected terminal points were both midway between troughs and peaks of cycles.[114]

For this project, this concern can be set aside since the banks included in this study were all affected by the same cycle. A geographically wider spread sample of banks might have altered this fact.

APPENDIX F

ANALYSIS OF VARIANCE

The design of the research requires the simultaneous study of several sub-groups of banks. The reasons for selecting the analysis of variance as the appropriate statistical procedure for this study were explained in Chapter IV. This Appendix will illustrate the rationale of the analysis of variance, the statistical technique employed, and the nature of the conclusions that can be drawn from the testing.

Although literally a technique which analyzes or tests variances, the analysis of variance permits the test of whether the means of b (where b is larger than 2) subsamples, into which the sample data are broken, are significantly different from each other. To illustrate the rationale of a test of variances and the computational procedures that are necessary, the first Hypothesis of this study will be examined and analyzed in detail. H_{1A}: Banks of size 'A' do not engage in significantly more long range planning (LRP) than do banks of size 'B.' H_{1B}: Banks of size 'B' do not engage in significantly more LRP than do banks of size 'C.' Bank size (large, medium, and small) and extent of long range planning (high, moderate, and low) were explained earlier. A total of 77 banks answered the portion of the questionnaire relating to the long range planning activities. Nine of the banks were large, 29 of medium size, and 21 were small. The mean LRP-Scores for the banks in the three size classes are presented in Table F-1.

LRP-SCORE
LRP-SCORE
LRP-SCORE

Table F-1

Mean LRP-Scores for Banks in Classes A, B, and C

Bank Class	A	B	C
Mean ($\bar{X}$)	31.615 ($\bar{X}_1$)	23.147 ($\bar{X}_2$)	26.367 ($\bar{X}_3$)

$$\text{Grand Mean } (\bar{\bar{X}}) = \frac{31.615 + 23.147 + 26.367}{3} = 25.831$$

The Hypothesis to be Tested

The mean LRP-Scores for the three bank classes are calculated as

$$\overline{X}_1 = 31.615$$
$$\overline{X}_2 = 23.147$$
$$\overline{X}_3 = 26.367$$

The statistical question to be answered is, can the three samples represented by these three means be considered as having been drawn from populations having the same means and variances?

The null hypothesis is stated as

$$H_o: \mu_1 = \mu_2 = \mu_3$$

where μ_1, μ_2, and μ_3 are the population means corresponding to $\overline{X}_1$, $\overline{X}_2$, and $\overline{X}_3$. The above hypothesis will be tested against the alternative hypothesis.

H_1: The three means μ_1, μ_2, and μ_3 are not all equal.

In essence, the objective of the test is to determine whether the differences among the sample means $\overline{X}_1$, $\overline{X}_2$, and $\overline{X}_3$ are too great to attribute to the chance errors of drawing samples from populations having the same mean. If the sample means differ significantly, the conclusion is that the extent to which banks engage in long range planning varies with bank size. (The assumptions underlying the test procedure were set forth in Chapter IV.)

Decomposition of Total Variation

If the null hypothesis that the three population means, μ_1, μ_2, and μ_3 are equal, is true, then both the variation among the sample means $\overline{X}_1$, $\overline{X}_2$, and $\overline{X}_3$ and the variation within the three groups reflect chance errors of the sampling process. To follow accepted terminology, these types of variation will be referred to as

"variation between groups"

and the second type will be referred to as

"variation within groups."

Between groups variation refers to variations of the sample means X_1, X_2, and X_3 around the grand mean, X. Within groups variation refers to the differences of the individual observations within each group from their respective means X_1, X_2, and X_3.

If the population means are equal, as hypothesized (H_0), the between groups variation and the within groups variation would be expected not to differ significantly from one another, since they both reflect the same type of chance sampling errors. If the null hypothesis is false, and the population group means are indeed different, than the between groups variation should significantly exceed the within groups variation. This follows from the fact that the between groups variation would be produced by the inherent differences among the group means as well as by chance sampling errors. The within groups variation would still reflect chance sampling errors only. Therefore, a comparison of between groups variation and within groups variation results in information concerning differences among the group means.[115]

The term "variation," as used in the statistical discussions of this project, refers to a sum of squared deviations and is called "sum of squares." A measure of variation divided by an appropriate number of degrees of freedom results in a "variance." In the analysis of variance, such a variance is commonly referred to as a "mean square."

> The variation of a set of sample observations, denoted X, around their mean X is Σ $(X-X)^2$. Dividing this sum of squares by the number of degrees of freedom n-1, where n is the number of observations, we obtain [Σ $(X-X)^2$] / (n-1), the sample variance, which is an unbiased estimator of the population variance. This sample variance can also be referred to as a "mean square."[116]

Between Groups Variation

As explained earlier, the between groups variation measures the variation among the sample group means. The variation, or between groups sum of squares, is calculated as follows:

$$\text{Between groups sum of squares} = \sum_j b\,(\bar{X}_j - \bar{\bar{X}})$$

where b = number of banks (sample size in the calculation of each group mean: $\bar{X}_1$ = 31.615, $\bar{X}_2$ = 23.147, $\bar{X}_3$ = 26.367); $\bar{X}$ = the means of the jth group (groups $\bar{X}_1$, $\bar{X}_2$, $\bar{X}_3$); $\bar{\bar{X}}$ = the grand mean ($\bar{\bar{X}}$ = 25.831); $\sum_j$ = indicates that the summation is taken over all groups.

The computation of the between groups sum of squares for the first hypothesis (examining the relationship of bank size and the extent of long range planning) is presented in Table F-2. As indicated, the between groups variation is equal to 688.46.

Table F-2

Calculation of the Between Groups Sum of Squares of LRP-Scores for Banks of Sizes A, B, and C.

$(\bar{X} - \bar{\bar{X}})^2$	=	(31.615 - 25.831)	=	33.454656
$(\bar{X} - \bar{\bar{X}})^2$	=	(23.147 - 25.831)	=	7.203856
$(\bar{X} - \bar{\bar{X}})^2$	=	(26.367 - 25.831)	=	0.287296
$\sum_j^b (\bar{X}_j - \bar{\bar{X}})^2$	=	13 (33.455) + 34 (7.204) + 30 (0.287) =		
	=	688.46		

Within Groups Variation

The within groups variation measures the sum of the random errors of the individual observations around their group means. The variation, or within groups sum of squares, is calculated as follows:

$$\text{Within groups sum of squares} = \sum_j \sum_i (X_{ij} - \bar{X})^2$$

where X_{ij} = the LRP-Score of the ith bank in the jth size class (class A, B, or C); X_j = the mean of the jth group (X_1, X_2, or X_3); $\sum_j \sum_i$ = the squared deviations are first summed over all sample observations within a given group and then summed over all groups.

The computation of the within groups sum of squares for the first hypothesis is presented in Table F-3 below. As indicated in the table, the within groups variation is equal to 12294.339.

Number of Degrees of Freedom

As stated earlier, if a measure of variation, such as a sum of squares, is divided by the appropriate number of degrees of freedom, the resulting measure is a variance (a mean square). The determination of the number of degrees of freedom associated with each of the measures of variation computed for Hypothesis No. 1 is described below.

The number of degrees of freedom associated with the between groups sum of squares is

$$g - 1$$

where g denotes the number of groups, e.g., size A, size B, and size C. Since the testing of Hypothesis No. 1 comprises 'g' (3) group means, 'g' sums of squares are involved in measuring the variation of these group means around the grand mean. Because the sample grand mean is only an estimation of the unknown population mean, one degree of freedom is lost. The number of degrees of freedom for the between groups sum of squares for Hypothesis No. 1 is

$$g - 1 = 3 - 1 = 2$$

The number of degrees of freedom associated with the within groups sum of squares is

$$(b_1 + b_2 + b_3) - g$$

where b_1 is the number of banks in size class A, b_2 the number of banks in size class B, and b_3 the number of banks in size class C.

From the sample grand mean, $\overline{\overline{X}}$, $b_1 + b_2 + b_3$ squared deviations are computed. Since $\overline{\overline{X}}$ is an estimate of the true but unknown population mean, one degree of freedom is lost. The number of degrees of freedom for the within groups sum of squares for the testing of Hypothesis No. 1 is

$$[(b_1 + b_2 + b_3) - g] = 13 + 34 + 30 - 3 = 74$$

In the determination of the total sum of squares, $b_1 + b_2 + b_3$ squared deviations are computed. Of the degrees of freedom, $(b_1 + b_2 + b_3) - 1$ may be arbitrarily assigned, but the last degree of freedom is constrained in order for the sum to be equal to the number of degrees of freedom for the total sum of squares.

The number of degrees of freedom associated with the total variation is $b_1 + b_2 + b_3 - 1 = 13 + 34 + 30 - 1 = 76$. The number of degrees of freedom associated with the between and within groups variations are equal to the number associated with the total variation.

Table F-3

Calculation of the Within Groups Sum of Squares of LRP-Scores for Banks of Sizes A, B, and C.

i	$(X_{i1} - \overline{X}_1)$			$(X_{i1} - \overline{X}_1)^2$
1	(38 - 31.615)	=	6.385	40.768
2	(41 - 31.615)	=	9.385	88.078
3	(42 - 31.615)	=	10.385	107.848
.				.
.				.
.				.
13	(41 - 31.615)	=	9.385	88.078
				1879.086

i	$(X_{i2} - \overline{X}_2)$			$(X_{i2} - \overline{X}_2)^2$
1	(34 - 23.147)	=	10.853	117.787
2	(41 - 23.147)	=	17.853	318.729
3	(35 - 23.147)	=	11.853	140.493
.				.
.				.
.				.
34	(35 - 23.147)	=	11.853	140.493
				6238.273

i	$(X_{i3} - \overline{X}_3)$			$(X_{i3} - \overline{X}_3)^2$
1	(37 - 26.367)	=	10.633	113.060
2	(38 - 26.367)	=	11.633	135.326
3	(44 - 26.367)	=	17.633	310.922
.				.
.				.
.				.
30	(33 - 26.367)	=	6.633	43.996
				4176.980

$$\sum_j \sum_i (X_{ij} - \overline{X}_j)^2 = 1879.086 + 6238.273 + 4176.98 = $$
$$= \underline{12294.339}$$

$$(b_1 + b_2 + b_3) - 1 = (g - 1) + [(b_1 + b_2 + b_3) - g]$$
$$76 = (3 - 1) + [(13 + 34 + 30) - 3]$$
$$= 2 + 74$$

The Analysis of Variance Table

Table F-4 presents an analysis of variance table for LRP-Scores for banks of Sizes A, B, and C. The table is designed to summarize the results of the analysis of variance. Columns (1), (2), and (3), respectively, list the possible sources of variation, the sum of squares for each of these sources, and the number of degrees of freedom associated with each of the sum of squares.

Adding sums of squares and numbers of degrees of freedom for between groups and within groups variations together, result in corresponding figures for the total variation. Dividing the sum of squares in Column (2) by the number of degrees of freedom in Column (3), yields the between groups and within groups mean square. For the analysis of Hypothesis No. 1, the between group mean square (MS_b) is equal to

$$\frac{688.4805}{2} = 344.3402$$

The within groups mean square (MS_w) is equal to

$$\frac{12294.3398}{74} = 166.1397$$

The test of the null hypothesis, that the sub-population group means are equal, is carried out by comparing MS_b to MS_w.

The F-Test

Between group mean square (MS_b) and within group mean square (MS_w) are compared by computing the F-ratio as follows:

$$F = \frac{MS_b}{MS_w}$$

If the null hypothesis is true that the population group means, $\overline{X}_1$, $\overline{X}_2$, and $\overline{X}_3$ are equal, the F-ratio would tend to be equal to 1. If the population group means do differ, the between groups mean square,

Table F-4

Analysis of Variance Table of LRP-Scores for Banks of Sizes A, B, and C.

LRP - SCORE

LRP - SCORE

LRP - SCORE

$H_{1A,B}$

(1) SOURCE OF VARIATION	(2) SUM OF SQUARES	(3) DEGREES OF FREEDOM	(4) MEAN SQUARE
Between Groups	688.4805	(2)	344.3402
Within Groups	12294.3398	(74)	166.1397
Total	12982.8203	(76)	

$$F(2,74) = \frac{344.3402}{166.1397} = 2.072$$

Critical F-value (5% level of significance)

$F(2,74) = 3.13$

MS_b, will tend to exceed the within groups mean square, MS_w, and the F-ratio will be greater than 1.

If F is large (the criterion of the exact size of the test statistic F are the critical values of the F-ratio which are tabulated in tables for frequently used significance levels), the null hypothesis that the population group means are all equal (H_o: $\mu_1 = \mu_2 = \mu_3$) will be rejected. If F is close to 1, the null hypothesis will be accepted.

Any standard table of critical values of the F-ratio indicates that the critical value for F with 2 degress of freedom for MS_b (numerator) and 74 degrees of freedom for MS_w (denominator) at the 5% level of statistical significance is equal to 3.13. (The figure was computed through interpolation by using tables in Dixon and Massey.)[117]

$$F.05(2,74) = 3.13$$

Since the computed value (see Table F-4) is equal to 2.072, and, therefore, smaller than the critical value of 3.13, the null hypothesis cannot be rejected. The conclusion of the testing of Hypothesis No. 1 is that the group sample means, LRP-Scores for banks of sizes A, B, and C, are not significantly different from each other. The inference about the corresponding population means are that the means are all the same.

APPENDIX G

SURVEY OF LRP PRACTICES

Studies during the 1960's (refer to Chapter II for details), notably Olson (1964) and Hegazy (1965), suggested the use of profit planning and long range planning techniques in commercial banks. One objective of this study is to determine how and to what extent long range planning is used in commercial banks a decade after these proposals were made.

Data on the extent of long range planning activities undertaken by commercial banks were collected through the use of the questionnaire. The same questionnaire also served as the instrument to collect growth and profit data on banks. Furthermore, the questionnaire solicited demographical information on participating commercial banks.

Questions pertaining to long range planning served to determine the extent to which the participating commercial banks engage in long range planning. As explained in previous chapters (refer to Chapters I and IV), answers to specific areas of inquiry of the questionnaire were the basis for the computation of "LRP-Scores." These "LRP-Scores" then permitted the classification of the participating banks according to the research-partition-design.

In the following section, information from the questionnaires is used to summarize long range planning practices of commercial banks of the 7th Federal Reserve Bank district. Some demographical data are presented first.

Demographics

Questionnaires were mailed to 144 commercial banks of the 7th Federal Reserve district to collect data on the long range planning practices. Seventy-seven commercial banks (53%) responded to the mailing. All answers were usable for the survey part of the study.

The surveyed banks are from the following five states: Illinois (43%), Indiana (8%), Iowa (21%), Michigan (15%), and Wisconsin (13%). When categorized by size (according to the criteria discussed in Chapter I and IV), 17% of the banks are considered to be large (Size A), 44% are of medium size (Size B), and 39% of the banks are small (Size C).[118]

Of the responding banks 75% have a national charter, 25% have a state charter, 12% are one-bank holding and 21% are multi-bank holding companies. Only 28% of the surveyed banks have branches (domestic).

This result was expected since Illinois is a unit bank state and 43% of all sampled banks are located in Illinois.

The banks have trading areas as follows:

up to 25,000	- 16%
between 25,000 and 100,000	- 33%
between 100,000 and 500,000	- 48%

The majority of banks serve rural, suburban and urban areas. Only 4% of the surveyed banks have a national clientele. Locally dominant industries exercise the following influence on the responding banks' "fortunes."

strong influence	- 14%
moderate influence	- 26%
little influence	- 60%

The number of years the chief executive officer of each bank has been managing the affairs of the bank is almost equally divided into three groups: banks where the executive has held the position up to 4 years, between 4 to 10 years and more than 10 years.

Ten percent of the banks control an overall share of their "local banking market" of up to 10%, 18% control between 10% and 25%, 29% between 25% and 40%, and 40% of the banks control more than 40% of the "local market." The strongest concentration of market share occurs among banks whose dependency on one dominant industry is low. Twenty-five percent of all banks fall into this category. Eighty percent of the locally dominant banks (40% and more of the "local market") engage in LRP to high or moderate extent. Of the banks that control between 25% and 40% of their "local market," 73% engage in LRP to high or moderate extent. The strong correlation between extent of LRP efforts undertaken by a bank and the control of the "local market" clearly indicates that LRP played an important role in achieving market dominance.

The analysis of the data revealed that small and medium banks control a much larger share of their markets than large banks. Thirty-nine percent of all sampled banks are small. One half of these small banks are very dominant in their market (40% and more of "local market"). Another 27% of these banks are moderately dominant (25% to 40% of "local market"). Forty-four percent of all sampled banks are of medium size. Thirty-eight percent of these banks are very dominant and 29% are moderately dominant in their "local market." Only 23% of the large banks are very dominant.

At first glance these findings seem to be contrary to expectations. Large banks are generally believed to be in a stronger position to achieve dominant market position. A possible explanation for these data is the fact that many communities do not generate enough business to sustain many commercial banks.

Corporate Goals

To determine the importance banks attach to different corporate goals, the respondents were asked to indicate the importance these goals have in their respective banks. (The set of goals was developed from the banking literature.) The answers are summarized in Table G-1 below.

Table G-1

Corporate Goals

	Importance attached by Bank		
	High	Moderate	Low
Adequate Profit	90%	10%	0%
Growth	34%	56%	10%
Customer Satisfaction	94%	6%	0%
Community Service	46%	47%	7%
Staff Development	48%	48%	4%
Capital Adequacy	10%	10%	0%
Stock Price	3%	0%	0%

Adequate profits and customer satisfaction achieved the highest priorities. Growth, a key variable under examination in this study, is considered of high importance by one third of the banks, while more than half of the banks indicate a moderate interest in growth. Although Capital Adequacy is a topic that is widely discussed in banking and financial circles, only 20% of all responding banks indicated special attention to this goal. This apparent contradiction reflects the fact that most bankers consider this goal beyond their control because capital adequacy is largely prescribed and controlled by law.

Ranking of the corporate goals (1 = most important, 5 = least important) resulted in Table G-2. Again, the surveyed banks considered adequate profits as the single most important goal requiring their attention. Customer satisfaction is the most often cited goal, with the second highest priority, followed by growth and staff development as having priorities three and four. Community service takes on the approximately same importance as staff development.

These data confirm the findings of the literature review regarding the importance of adequate profits and satisfactory growth performance. The high ranking of customer satisfaction must be seen as the rising awareness and response on the part of bankers to consumer activism.

Table G-2

Ranking of Corporate Goals

GOALS	RANK 1	2	3	4	5
Adequate Profit	68%	16%	13%	5%	-
Growth	9%	14%	43%	17%	18%
Customer Satisfaction	19%	44%	18%	12%	5%
Community Service	4%	18%	10%	27%	39%
Staff Development	-	8%	14%	39%	37%
No Ranking	-	-	-	-	1%
	100%	100%	100%	100%	100%

Planning Horizon

The majority of banks consider a three year planning horizon for long range planning in banks as most advisable (42% - 3 years, 17% - 2 years, 16% - more than 4 years, 13% - 4 years, 5% - 1 year). Banks with low (10% to 25% of "local market"), moderate (25% to 40%), and strong dominance of their "local banking market" advocating a three year planning horizon represent 10%, 12%, and 40% of all respondents, respectively. Furthermore, banks with a "market share" of more than 40% suggesting 4 and 5 year time frames for long range planning, represent another 7% and 12% of all banks. When bank size is considered, the results are similar. Fifty-four percent of all large banks, 35% of all medium banks, and 43% of all small banks consider three years as the appropriate planning horizon for long range planning in commercial banks.

Long Range Planning Activities

Data Analysis reveals that all responding banks engage in some long range planning activities, although only 71% of the banks responded positively to a direct question concerning their own long range planning.

Eighty-eight percent of the banks prepare written budgets covering a time span of up to one year. Pro forma Balance Sheet (83%) and Income Statement (82%) are very often part of these budgets. The Statement of Sources and Uses of Funds (= Statement of Changes in Financial Position) does not enjoy the same widespread acceptance (only 36%) as the former two statements.

Working standards for employees (e.g., guidelines concerning processing-time of loans) are prepared by 20% of the respondents (61% of large banks, 9% of medium banks and 13% of small banks). Forty percent of all respondents have a profit planning program (where overall expected profit contributions from each functional area are developed). Eighty-four percent of all large banks, 50% of all medium banks and 40% of all small banks report to have this type of profit planning program.

In most banks long range planning activities are the responsibility of top management (70%). Slightly less than half of the responding banks started with LRP during or before 1972 (43%). Pro forma Balance Sheet, Income Statement, and the Statement of Sources and Uses of Funds are part of LRP in 87% (83%), 84% (82%), and 35% (36%) of the banks, respectively. Percentages in parentheses represent the frequency of preparation of these reports for one year budgets of all responding banks. (Refer to discussion above.) Two thirds of all banks engaging in long range planning activities prepare formalized (written) projections, while one third engages in only oral discussion of future plans.

The following objectives are part of long range plans as reported by the banks. The numbers in parentheses indicate the number of years into the future these plans are projected.

Corporate objectives - (e.g., strategic plans). Sixty four percent of the banks make forecasts as follows: 2 years - 12%, 3 years - 21%, 5 years - 31%.

Capital Funds - 66% of the banks make forecasts for this objective (25% - 4 years, 18% - 3 years, 16% - 2 years).

Fixed Assets - 66% of the banks make forecasts for fixed assets (5% - 3 years, 21% - 5 years, 17% - 2 years).

Investments - 62% make forecasts (22% - 4 years, 17% - 2 years, 16% - 3 years).

Volume of deposits - 70% of all banks make forecasts (25% - 2 years, 22% - 3 years, 21% - 5 years). By deposit category, forecasts are made by 65% of the banks (26% - 2 years, 21% - 3 years, 16% - 5 years).

Volume of loans - 71% of the banks attempt to predict the volume of loans (27% - 2 years, 23% - 3 years, 18% - 5 years). By loan category, the forecasts are made by 66% of the banks (27% - 2 years, 20% - 3 years, 14% - 5 years).

Manpower planning and control - 54% of all banks make forecasts for manpower and control (21% - 3 years, 17% - 2 years, 16% - 5 years).

Staff Training - Only 43% of the responding banks include staff training in their LRP (25% - 2 years, 12% - 3 years, 6% - 5 years).

Product Planning and Advertising - (new services and improvements, etc.). Fifty-two percent of all banks make product plans (31% - 2 years, 14% - 3 years, 7% - 5 years). The percentage for product advertising and promotion is 42% (31% - 2 years, 8% - 3 years, 3% - 5 years).

Bank-image - 48% of all banks make plans for bank-image advertising and promotion (34% - 2 years, 9% - 3 years, 5% - 5 years).

Organizational Structure - An even 50% of the banks surveyed include organizataional structure and development planning in the long range forecasts (20% - 3 years, 16% - 2 years, 14% - 5 years).

Other - Interaction between functional areas, departments and/or branches, competitor action and market share planning concern 23%, 33%, and 40% of all banks.

Outside expertise to assist in LRP-activities is rarely sought. Research firms, independent professionals, and consulting firms (including CPA's) are called upon only by 5%, 17%, and 10% of the banks respectively. Banks make, however, extensive use of the following sources of information:

Government Agencies (e.g., Federal Reserve Bank, Commerce Department) - 66%

Experts on future business conditions (e.g., economists) - 61%
Magazines (e.g., *Fortune, Economist, Newsweek*) - 53%
Newspaper reports (e.g., *Wall Street Journal, New York Times*) - 51%.

The above sources of information are used to identify developments in the following areas:

Economic trends - 55%
Population trends - 39%
Technological breakthroughs - 30%
Growth of money supply - 29%
Personal incomes - 21%
Political developments - 13%
Social currents - 12%
Labor-Management relations - 8%

Planning Approaches

Among the most widely used planning techniques are predictions based on recurring business cycles (56% of all banks). Forecasts made by the correspondent bank are often used (46%). Many bankers look for and rely on the prediction of key elements, rather than making comprehensive studies of the entire economy (38%). Interest rates, because of their immediate impact on profit, also rank high in planning activities. Thirty percent of the surveyed bankers attempt to predict Federal Authorities' policies that might affect interest rates. Many bankers simply base their prediction of future activities on the assumption of the continuation of current business conditions, a technique that is sometimes referred to as naive forecast (30%). Reliance on patterns of relationship of various economic activities finds application too (27%). If, for example, it is possible to predict important segments, it may be possible to predict the whole structure by relying on past relationships. Use of "lead series" (such as economic indicators used by Commerce and Labor Department), developed from past movements in economic activities to predict future developments, are slightly less popular (25%). Some bankers (17%) survey present plans of industrial leaders in key positions in industry to uncover and predict what will happen between now and the time those plans are completed and how these developments might affect their bank now and then.

Few banks (12%) have an economist on the staff who participates in forecasting. Computers are used only sparingly in LRP (13%).

Econometric models for LRP find application only in a few banks (5%). Sometimes (10%) bankers compare a list of all favorable factors with a list of all unfavorable factors in making predictions.

The overwhelming majority (95%) prepare LRP on an annual basis. The frequency of up dating these plans, however, varies among the banks. Quarterly, semi-annual, and annual updating is common in 17%, 16%, and 57% of the banks respectively.

Support for LRP by top management ranges from very strong (31%), strong (52%), to occasionally (17%). The reasons for engaging in LRP are diverse and receive differing degrees of attention. Some important reasons (with percentages of responses) are listed below:

To avoid decline in profit (56%)
Increased size and complexity of business (53%)
Increased competition (44%)
Chief-executive encourages LRP (35%)
Increased variety and number of services offered (29%)
Decreased Interest margin (26%).

The most important reason for not engaging in LRP is staffing problems (14%). Lacking management support (10%) and amount of time required to prepare the LRP (9%) are other reasons cited for not engaging in LRP activities. Less important reasons mentioned are:

Not accurate enough (5%)
Environmental conditions are not predictable (4%)
Necessary information is not available or not quantifiable (4%)
Lack of proven success (3%)
Lack of planning guides (1%).

NOTES

[1]Levis D. McCullers and Relmond P. Van Daniker, *Introduction to Financial Accounting* (Los Angeles, California: Melville Publishing Company, 1975), p. 395.

[2]Hashem Mohammed Ali Sabbagh. "The Utilization of Selected Managerial Accounting Concepts and Techniques in Branch Bank Management" (unpublished Ph.D. dissertation, The University of Arizona, 1971), p. 267.

[3]See Table II-1.

[4]Staff Report on *Concentration of Banking in the United States* of the Board of Governors of the Federal Reserve System to the *Subcommittee on Monopoly of the Select Committee on Small Business, United States Senate* (Washington, D.C.: U.S. Government Printing Office, 1952), p. 1.

[5]Ronald L. Olson. "Profit Planning in Commercial Banks" (unpublished Ph.D. dissertation, Indiana University, 1964), p. 1.

[6]Roy L. Reierson, "Economic Analysis: A Basis for Profit Planning," *Auditgram* (January, 1964), p. 6.

[7]Olson, "Profit Planning in Commercial Banks," p. xiii.

[8]*Ibid.*

[9]Leonard Laudadio. "The Adequacy of Bank Profits" (unpublished Ph.D. dissertation, University of Washington, 1960), p. 1.

[10]Paul V. Teplitz, *Trends Affecting the U.S. Banking System* (Cambridge, Massachusetts: Ballinger Publishing Company, 1976), p. 161.

[11]Laudadio, "The Adequacy of Bank Profits," p. 99.

[12]Haskins & Sells, *Bank Cost for Planning and Control* (Park Ridge, Illinois: Bank Administration Institute, 1972), p. 3.

[13]Laudadio, "The Adequacy of Bank Profits," p. 1.

[14]United States Congress, Testimony of William McChesney Martin, Chairman, Board of Governors, Federal Reserve System, Hearings before the Joint Economic Committee, *Employment, Growth, and Price Levels,* Part 6A, "The Government's Management of its Monetary, Fiscal and Debt Operations," 86th Congress, 1st Session, July 1959, p. 1499.

[15]Burnard H. Sord and Glenn A. Welsch, *Business Budgeting, A Survey of Management Planning and Control Practices* (New York: The Controllership Foundation, 1958), p. 122.

[16]Olson, "Profit Planning in Commercial Banks," p. 9.

[17]Mohamed Hegazy, "An Application of Budgetary Control to Commercial Banks with Reference to the Principles of Commercial Bank Management" (unpublished Ph.D. dissertation, University of Wisconsin, 1965), p. 10.

[18]Adolph Matz, Othel J. Curry and George W. Frank, *Cost Accounting* (Cincinnati: South-Western Publishing Company, 1967), p. 2.

[19]George A. Steiner, "Making Long-Range Company-Planning Pay-off," *California Management Review* (Winter, 1962).

[20]For additional definitions of long-range planning refer to the following sources: George A. Steiner, "What Do We Know About Using Long-Range Plans?" *California Management Review* (Fall, 1959); Peter F. Drucker, "Long Range Planning, Challenge to Management Science," *Management Science* (April, 1959); Bruce Payne and James H. Kennedy, "Making Long-Range Planning Work," *The Management Review* (February, 1959); and William H. Newman and Charles E. Summer, Jr., *The Process of Management* (Englewood Cliffs, New Jersey: Prentice-Hall, 1961), pp. 430-436.

[21]Robert N. Anthony, John Dearden, and Richard F. Vancil, *Management Control Systems* (Homewood, Ill.: Richard D. Irwin, Inc. 1965), p. 92.

[22]Bank Administration Institute, *Successful Profit Planning for Banks* (Park Ridge, Illinois: Bank Administration Insitute, 1970), p. 28.

[23]Bank Administration Institute, *Profit Planning and Control* (Park Ridge, Illinois: Bank Administration Institute, 1959).

[24]Mohamed Abbas Hegazy and Edward J. Blakely, Jr., *An Application of Budgeting Control to Commercial Banks with Reference to the Principles of Commercial Bank Management* (Madison, Wisconsin: The University of Wisconsin Bureau of Business Research and Service, 1965).

[25]Bank Administration Institute, *Successful Profit Planning for Banks* (Park Ridge, Illinois: Bank Administration Institute, 1970), p. 3.

[26]Olson, "Profit Planning in Commercial Banks," p. 3.

[27]Robert M. Fulmer and Leslie W. Rue, *The Practice and Profitability of LRP* (Oxford, Ohio: Planning Executive Institute, 1973), p. 5.

[28]Harvey Bresler, *Money and Banking* (New York: College Notes, Inc., 1969), p. 31.

[29]Teplitz, *Trends Affecting the U.S. Banking System*, p. 13.

[30]*Ibid.*

[31]Olson, "Profit Planning in Commercial Banks," p. 1.

[32]Teplitz, *Trends Affecting the U.S. Banking System*, p. 2.

[33]Lucille Stringer Mayne, *The Effect of Federal Reserve System Membership on the Profitability of Illinois Banks, 1961-1963* (Philadelphia: Center for Research of the College of Business Administration, The Pennsylvania State University, 1967), p. 11.

[34]In general terms, the federal regulations relate to the types of activities of banks, while state regulations mostly affect the size and locations of banks or their branches.

[35]William Brown, *The Dual Banking System in the United States* (New York: The American Bankers Association, 1968), p. 61.

[36]Federal Deposit Insurance Corporation, *Annual Report-1975* (Washington, D.C., 1976), p. 138-140.

[37]Edwin Walter Kemmerer and Donald L. Kemmerer, *The ABC of the Federal Reserve System* (New York: Harper and Bros., 1950), p. 24.

[38]FDIC, *Annual Report-1975*, pp. 159-161.

[39]*Ibid.* p. 138.

[40]Brown, *The Dual Banking System in the U.S.*, p. 45.

[41]*Ibid.* p. 59.

[42]*Ibid.* p. 63.

[43]Stringer Mayne, *The Effect of Federal Reserve Membership on Profitability of Illinois Banks, 1961-1963.*

[44]For more details on concentration of banking in the United States refer to *Staff Report of the Board of Governors of the Federal Reserve System to the Subcommittee on Monopoly of the Select Committee on Small Business, U.S. Senate, Concentration in Banking in the U.S.* (Washington, D.C.: Government Printing Office, 1952).

[45]Editorial, "United States Opposes Plan of Nebraska Banks on Transfer System," *Wallstreet Journal*, March 8, 1977.

[46]This multiplier is the reciprocal of the fraction kept in reserve. If banks hold back 17 percent of each new deposit as reserve, the total money supply will be about six times the amount of reserves.

[47]Teplitz, *Trends Affecting the U.S. Banking System*, p. 33.

[48]Concerns about "Capital Adequacy" first arose in the 1950's. Refer to Laudadio, "Adequacy for Bank Profits."

[49]Refer to Table II-3.

[50]Teplitz, *Trends Affecting the U.S. Banking System*, p. 158.

[51]American Bankers Association, *Results of the 1972 National Automation Survey* (Washington, D.C.: 1972).

[52]Teplitz, *Trends Affecting the U.S. Banking System*, p. 155.

[53]Staff Report of the Select Committee on Small Business, Eighty-Sixth Congress, *Banking Concentration and Small Business* (Washington, D.C.: Government Printing Office, 1960)

[54]Staff Report of the Board of Governors of the FRS, *Concentration of Banking in the U.S.* to the Sub-committee on Monopoly of the Select Committee on Small Business, U.S. Senate (Washington, D.C.: Government Printing Office, 1952).

[55]At the present time, the Federal Reserve Bank of Boston is cooperating with the Deutsche Bundesbank (Central Bank of West Germany) and several German Universities to explore these possibilities.

[56]Personal interview on Nov. 5, 1976 with Theo Morss, Director and founder of the Program at the Federal Reserve Bank in Boston.

[57]Gene Cozart Lynch, "A Study of Profit Determinants, State Banks in Texas, 1948-1957" (unpublished Ph.D. dissertation, University of Texas, 1962).

[58]Stringer Mayne, *The Effect of Federal Reserve Membership on Profitability of Illinois Banks, 1961-1963*, p. 3.

[59]Analyses prepared by Regulatory Agencies.

[60]Item counts of transactions, such as number of checks cashed or loans processed during a particular reporting period, are used to develop schemes for cost-allocation.

[61]Federal Reserve Bank, An Explanatory Guide to the Calculations and Techniques Employed in the *Functional Cost Analysis* Report (Chicago, Illinois: Federal Reserve Bank, 1975), pp. 3-4.

[62]*Ibid.*

[63]*Ibid.*, p. 36.

[64]Haskins and Sells, *Banks Costs for Planning and Control* (Park Ridge, Illinois: Bank Administration Institute, 1972), p. 158.

[65]*Ibid.*, p. 159.

[66]*Ibid.*, p. 168.

[67]*Ibid.*, p. 174.

[68]*Ibid.*

[69]Federal Reserve Bank, *Functional Cost Analysis Program, 1975 Average Banks* (Federal Reserve Bank Chicago, Illinois, 1976), p. i.

[70]Philip J. Runkel and Joseph E. McGrath, *Research on Human Behavior* (New York: Holt, Rinehart and Winston, Inc., 1972), p. 183.

[71]*Ibid.*

[72]*Ibid.*

[73]Thomas G. Evans, "Foreign Exchange Risk Management at American Multinationals: Social Responsibility or Earnings Protection?" (paper presented at the International Seminar on Accounting, University of Illinois at Urbana-Champaign, Ill., March 24 - 26, 1977).

[74]Olson, "Profit Planning in Commercial Banks," p. Xiii.

[75]Marshall E. Blume, "Risk and Investment Theory," *Journal of Finance*, XXVI. No. 1 (March, 1971), 1-10.

[76]Harvey Bresler, *Money and Banking* (New York, NY.: College Notes, Inc. 1969), p. 54. Also refer to Table IV-1 in this study.

[77]For a description of the boundaries of the 7th Federal Reserve district refer to note 105 in the section on limitations in this chapter.

[78]All data arrangements, modifications, computations and testing were done on IBM (system 360) computers at the University of Kentucky and at Boston University. Computer programs used included SPSS (Statistical Package for the Social Sciences - refer to Appendix B) and programs specifically designed for the analysis that follows.

[79]Changes in average deposits are used as surrogates for the measurement of growth. Refer to definition of growth in Appendix B.

[80]Changes in "Net Yield for Portfolio, Loans and Investments" are used as surrogates for the measurement of profit. Refer to definition of profit in Appendix B.

[81]Sidney Siegel, *Nonparametric Statistics* (New York: McGraw-Hill, 1956), p. 19.

[82]*Ibid.*, p. 19.

[83]*Ibid.*, p. 20.

[84]Olson, "Profit Planning in Commercial Banks," pp. 10-21.

[85]Neil v. Sunderland, *Bank Planning Models* (Bern: Verlag Paul Haupt, 1974), p. 19.

[86]According to the 1962 Annual Report of the FDIC, interest income accounted for 86.5 percent of total bank operating income, a trend that is confirmed by data in the Annual Reports for the years 1964-1973.

[87]Sunderland, *Bank Planning Models*, p. 150.

[88]Haskins & Sells, *Bank Costs for Planning and Control*, p. 157.

[89]Laudadio, "The Adequacy of Bank Profits," p. 109.

[90]T. W. Harris. "Budgetary Control for Commercial Banks" (unpublished thesis, Rutgers University, Stonier Graduate School of Banking, 1953), p. 46.

[91]Olson, "Profit Planning in Commercial Banks," p. 29.

[92]Sunderland, *Bank Planning Models*, pp. 11-12.

[93]Harris, "Budgetary Control for Commercial Banks," p. 47.

[94]Olson, "Profit Planning in Commercial Banks," p. 30.

[95]Refer to above "growth" and "profit" definitions and a more detailed description in Appendix B. For a discussion of the Functional Cost Analysis Program refer to Chapter III.

[96]Stringer Mayne, *The Effect of Federal Reserve System Membership on the Profitability of Illinois Banks, 1961-1963*, p. 84.

[97]Deborah Isaacs, *Changing Commercial Bank Structure in New England*, Research Report 59 Federal Reserve Bank of Boston, June 1975 (Boston, Mass.: Federal Reserve Bank of Boston, 1975), pp. 142-148.

[98]FDIC, Annual Reports.

[99]Olson, "Profit Planning in Commercial Banks," p. 29.

[100]Laudadio, "The Adequacy of Bank Profits," p. 109.

[101]Bank Administration Institute, *The 1974 BAI Index of Bank Performance* (Park Ridge, Ill.: BAI, 1975).

[102]Refer to definition on bank size in Appendix B.

[103]Regulatory reporting requirements changed, effective with the years 1969 and 1975.

[104]Bresler, *Money and Banking*, p. 54.

[105]Territory in District - State of Iowa, all that part of Wisconsin in the counties of Vernon, Monroe, Jackson, Clark, Marathon, Langlade, Oconto, and Marinette, together with all the counties lying east and south of these counties: all of the southern peninsula of Michigan, viz.: the part east of Lake Michigan: all that part of Illinois located north of a line forming the southern boundary of the following counties: Hancock, Schuyler, Cass, Sangamon, Christian, Shelby, Cumberland, and Clark; and all the part of Indiana north of a line forming the southern boundaries of the following counties: Vego, Clay, Owen, Monroe, Brown, Bartholomew, Jennings, Ripley, and Ohio. Source: Rand McNally International Bankers Directory, Final 1975 Edition, p. P 17.

[106]Wilfrid J. Dixon and Frank J. Massey, Jr. *Introduction to Statistical Analysis* (New York, N.Y.: McGraw-Hill Book Company, 1969), pp. 287-289.

[107]Federal Reserve Bank, *An Explanatory Guide to the Calculations and Techniques in the Functional Cost Analysis Report* (Federal Reserve Bank of Chicago, 1975), p. 1.

[108]Hereafter stated as (F2,74).

[109]Bank Administration Institute, *Successful Profit Planning for Banks,* pp. 30-31.

[110]Federal Reserve Bank, "*An Explanatory Guide to the Calculations and Techniques Employed in the Functional Cost Analysis Report.*"

[111]Norman H. Nie, C. Hadlai Hull, Jean G. Jenkins, Karin Steinbrenner, and Dale H. Bent, *SPSS-Statistical Package for the Social Sciences* (New York, N.Y.: McGraw-Hill Book Company, 1975), p. XXi.

[112]Morris Hamburg, *Statistical Analysis for Decision Making* (New York: Harcourt, Brace and World, Inc., 1970) pp. 180-181.

[113]*Ibid.*

[114]*Ibid.*

[115]Hamburg, *Statistical Analysis for Decision Making,* p. 441.

[116]*Ibid.*

[117]Dixon and Massey, *Introduction to Statistical Analysis,* p. 482.

[118]All percentages quoted from here on are based on 77 responses, unless indicated otherwise.

SELECTED BIBLIOGRAPHY

Agthe, Klaus. *Strategie und Wachstum der Unternehmung.* Baden-Baden: Verlag fuer Unternehmensfuehrung Dr. Max Gehlen, 1972.

American Bankers Association. *Results of the 1972 National Automation Survey.* Washington, D.C.: 1972.

American Management Association. *How Companies Plan.* New York, N.Y.: American Management Association, 1962.

Andrews, Frank M.; Klem, Laura; Davidson, Rerrence N.; O'Malley, Patrick M.; and Rodgers, Willard L. *A Guide for Selecting Statistical Techniques for Analyzing Social Science Data.* Ann Arbor, Michigan: Institute for Social Research, The University of Michigan, 1974.

Anthony, Robert N.; Dearden, John; and Vancil, Richard F. *Management Control Systems.* Homewood, Ill.: Richard D. Irwin, Inc. 1965.

Argenti, John. *Die Langfristplanung im Unternehmen.* Muenchen: Verlag Moderne Industrie, Wolfgang Dummer & Co., 1970.

Bank Administration Institute. *Profit Planning and Control.* Park Ridge, Ill.: Banks Administration Institute, 1959.

________. *Successful Profit Planning for Banks.* Park Ridge, Ill.: Banks Administration Institute, 1970.

________. *The 1974 BAI Index of Bank Performance.* Park Ridge, Ill.: Banks Administration Institute, 1975.

Blume, Marshall E. "Risk and Investment Theory." *Journal of Finance,* XXVI. No. 1 (March, 1971), 1-10.

Board of Governors of the Federal Reserve System. *Banking Studies.* Baltimore: Waverly Press, Inc., 1941.

Bresler, Harvey. *Money and Banking.* New York, N.Y.: College Notes, Inc., 1969.

Brown, William J. *The Dual Banking System in the United States.* New York: The American Bankers Association, 1968.

Bueschen, Hans E. "Zur Problematik dezentralisierter Bankunternehmensplanung." *Mitteilungen und Berichte des Institut's fuer Bankwirtschaft und Bankrecht,* 5. Jahrgang, Nr. 17, 1975, 5-34.

Campbell, Donald T., and Stanley, Julian C. *Experimental and Quasi-Experimental Designs for Research.* Chicago, Ill.: Rand McNally and Company, 1963.

Deppe, Hans-Dieter. *Bankbetriebliches Wachstum.* Stuttgart: J.B. Metzlersche Verlagsbuchhandlung und Carl Ernst Poeschel Verlag, GmbH, 1969.

Dixon, Wilfrid J., and Massey, Frank J. *Introduction to Statistical Analysis.* New York, N.Y.: McGraw-Hill Book Company, 1969.

Drucker, Peter F. "Long-Range Planning, Challenge to Management Science," *Management Science* (April, 1959).

Evans, Thomas G. "Foreign Exchange Risk Management at American Multinationals: Social Responsibility or Earnings Protection?" Paper presented at the International Seminar on Accounting, University of Illinois at Urbana-Champaign, Ill., March 24-26, 1977.

Federal Deposit Insurance Corporation. *Annual Reports.* Washington, D.C., 1961-1970.

Federal Reserve Bank. *An Explanatory Guide to the Calculations and Techniques Employed in the Functional Cost Analysis Report.* Federal Reserve Bank of Chicago, 1975.

________. *Functional Cost Analysis Program, 1975 Average Banks.* Federal Reserve Bank of Chicago, 1976.

________. *Functional Cost Analysis - 1973 Average Banks.* Washington, D.C., 1974.

Fulmer, Robert M., and Rue, Leslie W. *The Practice and Profitability of Long-Range Planning.* Oxford, Ohio: Planning Executive Institute, 1973.

Garcia, F.L. *How to Analyze a Bank Statement.* Boston: Bankers Publishing Company, 1974.

Guttentag, Jack M., and Herman, Edward S. *Banking Structure and Performance: A Summary and Appraisal of the Literature.* Philadelphia, Pennsylvania: Wharton School of Finance and Commerce, University of Pennyslvania, 1965.

Haeusler, Joachim. *Planung als Zukunftsgestaltung.* Wiesbaden: Dr. Th. Gabler Verlag, GmbH, 1969.

Hamburg, Morris. *Statistical Analysis for Decision Making.* New York, N.Y.: Harcourt, Brace & World, Inc., 1970.

Harris, T.W. "Budgetary Control for Commercial Banks." Unpublished Thesis, Rutgers University, Stonier Graduate School of Banking, 1953.

Haskins & Sells. *Bank Costs for Planning and Control.* Park Ridge, Ill.: Bank Administration Institute, 1972.

Hegazy, Mohamed. "An Application of Budgetary Control to Commercial Banks with Reference to the Principles of Commercial Bank Management." Unpublished Ph.D. dissertation, University of Wisconsin, 1965.

________, and Blakely, Edward J., Jr. *An Application of Budgeting Control to Commercial Banks with Reference to the Principles of Commercial Bank Management.* Madison, Wisconsin: The University of Wisconsin Bureau of Business Research and Service, 1965.

Henry, Harold W. "Formal Long-Range Planning and Corporation Performance." *The Michigan Business Review* (March, 1969), 24-31.

Isaacs, Deborah. *Changing Commercial Bank Structure in New England.* Research Report 59 Federal Reserve Bank of Boston, June 1975. Boston, Mass.: Federal Reserve Bank of Boston, 1975.

Kemmerer, Edwin Walter, and Kemmerer, Donald L. *The ABC of the Federal Reserve System.* New York: Harper and Bros., 1950.

Kohlbeck, Rosemarie. *Bankbetriebliche Plannung.* Wiesbaden: Verlag Dr. Th. Gabler, 1971.

Laudadio, Leonard. "The Adequacy of Bank Profits." Unpublished Ph.D. dissertation, University of Washington, 1960.

Leabo, Dick A. *Basic Statistics.* Homewood, Ill.: Richard D. Irwin, Inc., 1972.

Lindsay, William, and Rue, Leslie W. "The Impact of Environmental Complexity on the Long-Range Planning Process." Unpublished manuscript, Planning Executive Institute, Oxford, Ohio, 1975.

Lynch, Gene Cozart. "A Study of Profit Determinants, State Banks in Texas, 1948-1957." Unpublished Ph.D. dissertation, University of Texas, 1962.

Mason, Robert D. *Statistical Techniques in Business and Economics.* Homewood, Ill.: Richard D. Irwin, Inc., 1967.

Matz, Adolph; Curry, Othel, J.; and Frank, George W. *Cost Accounting.* Cincinnati, Ohio: South-Western Publishing Company, 1967.

McCullers, Levis D., and Van Daniker, Relmond P. *Introduction to Financial Accounting.* Los Angeles: Melville Publishing Company, 1975.

Morss, Theo. private interview held at Federal Reserve Bank of Boston, 1976.

Newmann, William H., and Summer, Charles E., Jr. *The Progress of Management.* Englewood Cliffs, NJ.: Prentice-Hall, 1961.

Nie, Norman H.; Hull, C. Hadlai; Jenkins, Jean G.; Steinbrenner, Karin; and Bent, Dale H. *SPSS-Statistical Package for the Social Sciences.* New York, N.Y.: McGraw-Hill Book Company, 1975.

Olson, Ronald L. "Profit Planning in Commercial Banks." Unpublished D.B.A. dissertation, Indiana University, 1964.

Payne, Bruce, and Kennedy, James H. "Making Long-Range Planning Work." *The Management Review* (February, 1959).

Price Waterhouse & Co. *Successful Profit Planning for Banks.* Park Ridge, Ill.: Bank Administration Institute, 1970.

Reierson, Roy L. "Economic Analysis: A Basis for Profit Planning." *Auditgram* (January, 1964).

Rand McNally. *International Bankers Directory.* Chicago, Ill.: Rand McNally, 1975.

Runkel, Philip J., and McGrath, Joseph E. *Research on Human Behavior.* New York, N.Y.: Holt, Rinehart and Winston, Inc., 1972.

Sabbagh, Hashem. "The Utilization of Selected Managerial Accounting Concepts and Techniques in Branch Bank Management." Unpublished Ph.D. dissertation, The University of Arizona, 1971.

Siegel, Sidney. *Nonparametric Statistics.* New York: McGraw Hill, 1956.

Sord, Burnard H., and Welsh, Glenn A. *Business Budgeting, A Survey of Management Planning and Control Practices.* New York, N.Y.: The Controllership Foundation, 1958.

Stebler, Alex. *Wege zur Strategischen Planung der Unternehmung.* Frankfurt/M.: Peter Lang, 1973.

Stedry, Andrew. *Budget Control and Cost Behavior.* Englewood Cliffs, N.J.: Prentice-Hall, Inc., 1960.

Steiner, George A. "Making Long-Range Planning Pay Off." *California Management Review* (Winter, 1962).

________. "What Do We Know About Using Long-Range Plans?" *California Management Review* (Fall, 1959).

Stockton, John R., and Clark, Charles T. *Business & Economics Statistics.* Cincinnati, Ohio: South-Western Publishing Company, 1971.

Stringer Mayne, Lucille. *The Effect of Federal Reserve System Membership on the Profitability of Illinois Banks, 1961-1963.* Philadelphia: Center for Research of the College of Business Administration, The Pennsylvania State University, 1967.

Sunderland, v. Neil. *Bank Planning Models.* Bern: Verlag Paul Haupt, 1974.

Teplitz, Paul V. *Trends Affecting the U.S. Banking System.* Cambridge, Mass.: Ballinger Publishing Company, 1976.

Thomas, William E., Jr. *Readings in Cost Accounting,* Budgeting and Control. Cincinnati, Ohio: South-Western Publishing Company, 1968.

UKCC. *User's Guide.* Lexington, Ky.: University of Kentucky Computing Center, 1974.

U.S. Congress. Joint Economic Committee. *Employment, Growth, and Price Levels.* Testimony by William McChesney Martin, Chairman of Governors, Federal Reserve System, Part 6A, "The Government's Management of its Monetary, Fiscal and Debt Operations," 86th Congress, 1st Session, 1959.

________. Select Committee on Small Business. *Banking Concentration and Small Business.* 86th Congress, Washington, D.C.: Government Printing Office, 1960.

________. Senate Subcommittee on Monopoly of the Select Committee on Small Business. *Concentration of Banking in the United States,* by Board of Governors of the Federal Reserve System. Washington, D.C.: Government Printing Office, 1959.

Wall Street Journal. Editorial, March 8, 1977.

Weiskam, Juergen. *Methoden der Voraussage als Grundlage betrieblicher Planung.* Freiburg im Breisgau: Rudolf Jaufe Verlag, 1963.

Zinken, Ruediger. *Die Planung im Bankbetrieb unter besonderer Beruecksichtigung operationsanalytischer Loesungsversuche zur Optimalplanung des Aktiv-und Passivgeschaefts.* Koeln: Druck Wienand KG, 1974.

INDEX

why was she killed?

Keith Wainman

Matador
9 Priory Business Park
Kibworth Beauchamp
Leicestershire LE8 0RX, UK
Tel: (+44) 116 279 2299
Fax: (+44) 116 279 2277
Email: books@troubador.co.uk
Web: www.troubador.co.uk/matador

ISBN 978 1783064 915

British Library Cataloguing in Publication Data.
A catalogue record for this book is available from the British Library.

Typeset in Aldine by Troubador Publishing Ltd
Printed and bound in the UK by TJ International, Padstow, Cornwall

Matador is an imprint of Troubador Publishing Ltd